MARY KURTIN
LAURIE WELLMAN, EDITOR

Grammar Workbook
for the
TOEFL® Exam

4TH EDITION

THOMSON

ARCO

Australia • Canada • Mexico • Singapore • Spain • United Kingdom • United States

An ARCO Book

ARCO is a registered trademark of Thomson Learning, Inc., and is used herein under license by Peterson's.

About The Thomson Corporation and Peterson's

With revenues of US$7.2 billion, The Thomson Corporation (www.thomson.com) is a leading global provider of integrated information solutions for business, education, and professional customers. Its Learning businesses and brands (www.thomsonlearning.com) serve the needs of individuals, learning institutions, and corporations with products and services for both traditional and distributed learning.

Peterson's, part of The Thomson Corporation, is one of the nation's most respected providers of lifelong learning online resources, software, reference guides, and books. The Education Supersite[SM] at www.petersons.com—the Internet's most heavily traveled education resource—has searchable databases and interactive tools for contacting U.S.-accredited institutions and programs. In addition, Peterson's serves more than 105 million education consumers annually.

For more information, contact Peterson's, 2000 Lenox Drive, Lawrenceville, NJ 08648; 800-338-3282; or find us on the World Wide Web at www.petersons.com/about.

ISBN 0-7689-0782-9

Printed in the United States of America

10 9 8 7 6 5   07 06 05 04

Contents

Chapter 1   The TOEFL Test and the Structure Section   1

What is the TOEFL Test?....................................... 1
Format of the Structure Section of the TOEFL CBT...................... 2
Why Use This Book?... 3
Tips for TOEFL Test Takers..................................... 3
Seven Steps to Using this Book Successfully........................... 4
Abbreviations... 5

Chapter 2   The Diagnostic Test   7

Error Identification... 8
Sentence Completion.. 12
Error Key.. 14

Chapter 3   Modifiers   17

Adverbs Like *Only*.. 17
Split Infinitives.. 18
Dangling Modifiers... 19
Adjective/Adverb Confusion..................................... 21
Adjectives after Verbs of Sensation................................ 23
Noun Adjectives... 24
Hyphenated or Compound Adjectives............................... 26
Demonstratives.. 27
Few, *Little*, *Much*, and *Many*............................... 28
Cardinal and Ordinal Numbers.................................... 30
Sameness and Similarity.. 31
Comparatives... 33
Superlatives.. 35
Cause and Result... 37
Articles.. 39
Too, *Very*, and *Enough*..................................... 41
Negation... 43
Chapter Quiz.. 46
Error Keys.. 49

Chapter 4   Verbs   55

Tense 55
Time Clauses 56
Verbs of "Demand" 57
Wishes 59
Conditionals 60
Modals 62
Verbals 64
Past Participles 68
Present and Perfect Participles and Infinitives 71
Chapter Quiz 73
Error Keys 75

Chapter 5   Pronouns   79

Relative Pronouns 79
Personal Pronouns—Case 80
Who/Whom 83
Possessives 85
Faulty Reference 86
Person 88
Number 89
Those Modified 92
Chapter Quiz 94
Error Keys 95

Chapter 6   Basic Patterns   99

Indirect Objects 99
Order of Adverbs 100
Embedded Questions 103
To/For (Purpose) 105
Double Subjects 106
Clauses 107
Chapter Quiz 111
Error Keys 113

Chapter 7 Style 115

Voice. 115
Parallelism 117
Wordiness. 120
Substandard. 122
Usage 125
Words Often Confused, Group I. 129
Words Often Confused, Group II 133
Words Often Confused, Group III. 137
Correlative Conjunctions 139
Subject/Verb Agreement 141
Parts of Speech. 144
Prepositions (General Use) 146
Prepositions in Combinations 149
Chapter Quiz. 153
Error Keys 157

Chapter 8 Practice Tests 163

Practice Test 1 164
Practice Test 2 168
Practice Test 3 172
Error Keys 176

The TOEFL Test and the Structure Section

What is the TOEFL Test?

The Test of English as a Foreign Language (TOEFL) test is a standardized test of English proficiency that is offered in a computer-based format in most parts of the world. The computer-based format is known as the TOEFL CBT. The TOEFL CBT is an admission requirement at many American and Canadian colleges and universities for international students whose native language is not English. Although the TOEFL test is offered in the CBT format in many parts of the world, a paper-based test is still offered in some places, and is called the Supplemental Administration of the TOEFL, or the TOEFL PBT (paper-based test). You can't choose which version of the test to take (CBT or PBT). You must take the version that is offered in the area in which you live. Information on the TOEFL CBT and the TOEFL PBT can be found at www.toefl.org—the official test Web site provided by Educational Testing Service. On the site, you can determine which test is offered in your area, and you can download or request a mailing of the Information Bulletin for the version of the test that you are taking. You can also contact ETS via mail at:

Educational Testing Service
Rosedale Road
Princeton, New Jersey 08541 USA
Telephone: 609-921-9000
Fax: 609-734-5410
E-mail: etsinfo@ets.org

It is the student's responsibility to find out the admission requirements of any schools that he or she might apply to for admission. If the TOEFL test is required, you should plan to take the test as soon as possible to allow time for these schools to receive and evaluate your scores. The Information Bulletin contains an application form and detailed information on such topics as where tests are administered; when, where, and how to apply for the TOEFL test; what kind of identification is needed for the day of the test; and how and when test scores are received. The writers of the bulletin attempt to anticipate and answer any questions a student may have about the test and how to apply to take it. Read this bulletin carefully before filling out the application form. After applying for the TOEFL test, each applicant will receive a ticket of confirmation and a "Handbook for Examinees." These will arrive about a month before the test is scheduled. The handbook will contain detailed information about the uses of score results. There is no one "passing" score for the TOEFL test: Each college or university has its own policy. The TOEFL test is only one factor considered in determining admission to a particular institution. Of course, every student wants to do as well as possible on the test and should use every opportunity to improve his or her English-language skills in general.

Format of the Structure Section of the TOEFL CBT

The TOEFL CBT has three sections:

1. Listening Comprehension
2. Structure
3. Reading Comprehension

The paper-based test varies slightly from the CBT in terms of the names of the sections and the order in which the questions are presented. On the paper-based test, Section 2 is called Structure and Written Expression, and the two types of questions (sentence completion and error-identification) are presented in separate subsections. There are also variations in how to approach the test based on the differences between computer-based and paper-based tests. For example, on the CBT, once you have confirmed your answer in the first two sections, you cannot go back and change that answer. You must also answer every question, you cannot move on to the next question until you have confirmed your answer for the previous question. For a full description of the differences in the exams, visit the official TOEFL Web site at www.toefl.org, or you can purchase a more comprehensive guide, such as ARCO's *Master the TOEFL CBT*, published by Peterson's. However, the grammar rules you'll need to know to do well on either the CBT or PBT are the same. This book deals only with the Structure section of the TOEFL test. The Structure section is designed to test your knowledge of standard written English. As stated above, there are two types of Structure questions, each with their own directions.

Directions for Sentence Completion

Directions: In the Sentence Completion questions, one or more words are left out of each sentence. Under each sentence, you will see four words or phrases. Select the one word or phrase that completes the sentence correctly, then write it in the space provided in the book or on a separate sheet of paper.

Example

If I _____ John, I will give him your message.

(A) saw
(B) see
(C) would see
(D) will see

In Standard written English, the sentence should read, "If I see John, I will give him your message." Therefore, you should have selected choice (B).

Directions for Error Identification

Directions: For the Error Identification questions, each sentence contains four underlined words or phrases. Select the one word or phrase that must be changed in order for the sentence to be correct. Circle your answer in the book or mark your answer on a separate sheet of paper.

Example

Each of the students <u>were asked</u> to <u>be</u> on time for class on <u>Friday</u>.
　　　　　　(A)　　　(B) (C)　　　　　　　(D)

Choice (A) is not acceptable in standard written English. The subject of the verb is *Each*, which is singular. The verb should be *was asked*. Therefore, the sentence should read, "Each of the students was asked to be on time for class on Friday." You should have selected choice (A) as the correct answer.

Why Use this Book?

Several features make this workbook an excellent and efficient tool for preparing for the Structure section of the TOEFL test.

First is the advantage of having a diagnostic test at the beginning of the book. You should take this test as you start studying for the TOEFL test for two reasons: (1) to get a picture of your ability in the Structure section and (2) to pinpoint your strengths and weaknesses in grammar. This will enable you to go straight to the parts of the book that offer practice in the areas in which you have the most difficulty.

Second, this book has been designed to teach and simplify complex grammar as well as to provide practice with questions similar to those on the actual TOEFL test. This book contains grammatical explanations followed by simple correct-incorrect exercises that will help you recognize and master one point of grammar at a time. Chapter quizzes test all points covered in one chapter. Practice tests at the end of the book cover grammar concepts from the entire book. All exercises, quizzes, and practice TOEFL tests are keyed to specific points of grammar and the exact pages in this book where this material may be found.

Tips for TOEFL Test Takers

Plan your study schedule at least several weeks before the actual test. Don't expect to learn all the information in a few days. Study regularly. Here are some important points to remember when you take the TOEFL:

1. Keep track of the time. There will be a timer on your screen for the computer-based test. If you are taking the paper-based test, take a watch and keep track of the time being posted on the blackboard.

2. Guess if you do not know the answer. It will not count against you. No points are deducted from your score for incorrect answers. Your score is based on the number of questions you answer correctly. Therefore, you should answer every question—and on the CBT, you must answer each question, and you cannot go back and change your answers.

3. Follow all directions (either spoken, recorded, or written) to each section carefully.

4. On the CBT, make sure you have clicked on the correct answer before you click Confirm and move on—you cannot go back and change your answer. On the PBT, be careful to fill in each circle on the answer sheet completely. (The computer may not record your answer if the circle is not totally filled in.) Be sure not to fill in two answers for the same question.

5. Choose the *best* answer. Do not forget that more than one answer may appear grammatically correct, but only one will be the *best* choice.

6. Choose the answer that seems clearest and most concise.

7. Work as quickly as you can, but do not be careless.

Seven Steps To Using this Book Successfully

1. Take the Diagnostic Test.

2. Check your answers using the error key that follows the test. The error key gives the name of the grammatical point covered and the page number where review material can be found.

3. Study the specific grammatical points carefully. Do the exercise that follows each one. Check your answers using the error key, which refers you to a specific grammatical rule or note. In some cases, *but not in all*, the error keys contain more than one possible corrected answer. The error keys are located at the end of each chapter.

4. Take the chapter quizzes. Check your answers using the error keys, which refer you to grammatical points and page numbers for review.

5. Take Practice Tests 1, 2, and 3 at the end of the book. *Be sure to time yourself or have a friend time you*. Budget your time; work quickly but carefully.

6. Check your answers using the error keys that follow the tests. The error key will refer you to the grammatical point in question and the page number where it can be found.

7. Take the tests again, if necessary.

If you would like a more in-depth review of the entire TOEFL test, *Master the TOEFL CBT 2002*, published by Peterson's, is a comprehensive study tool that includes information and practice for both the CBT and the PBT. If you purchase the CD version of the book, you will have access to an online practice TOEFL test offered by Peterson's.

Abbreviations

The following is a list of the abbreviations used in the review sections of this book.

adj.	adjective
adv.	adverb
aux.	auxiliary
cl.	clause
CN	count noun
comp.	comparative
conj.	conjunction
d.o.	direct object
fut.	future
infin. (or *to* + *V*)	infinitive
i.o.	indirect object
irr.	irregular
N	noun
NCN	non-count noun
neg.	negative
obj.	object
part.	participle
past part.	past participle
past perf.	past perfect
perf. part.	perfect participle
pl.	plural
prep.	preposition
pres.	present
pron.	pronoun
QW	question word
S	subject
sing.	singular
suprl.	superlative
to + *have* + **past part.**	perfect infinitive
to + **V (or infin.)**	infinitive
V	simple form of the verb
V + *ing*	present participle or gerund

The Diagnostic Test

2

This diagnostic test will give you an idea of the kinds of grammatical points that will be tested in the Structure section of the TOEFL test. After you have taken the diagnostic test, check your answers with the error key on page 14. The error key lists the correct answer for each question and tells you where to find the review material for the grammatical point that is being tested. This diagnostic test will help identify the areas of English grammar that are most difficult for you. Then, you can turn to the discussions of specific grammatical points and begin studying to review and improve your knowledge of standard written English.

Read the directions carefully before you start the diagnostic test.

DIAGNOSTIC TEST

Time Allowed—40 minutes

Error Identification

Directions: For the Error Identification questions, each sentence contains four underlined words or phrases. Select the one word or phrase that must be changed in order for the sentence to be correct. Circle your answer in the book or mark your answer on a separate sheet of paper.

1. Beautiful is in the eye of the beholder.
   (A)   (B)   (C)   (D)

2. The baby showed a noticeable distaste for these kind of prepared baby food.
                       (A)   (B)   (C)   (D)

3. They cannot go camping right now because they are taking care of a three-weeks-old baby.
                          (A)   (B)   (C)   (D)

4. They went into the Superstition Mountains in search for the Lost Dutchman's Mine and were
              (A)   (B)
   never heard from again.
   (C)   (D)

5. The young girl dreamed a dream that she was being carried away by monsters.
                          (A)   (B)   (C)   (D)

6. If it will rain this afternoon, we will have to cancel the picnic.
   (A) (B)   (C)   (D)

7. Are you familiar of the latest scientific developments in the field?
   (A)   (B)   (C)   (D)

8. Henry is the sort of a man who will give you the shirt off his back.
              (A)   (B)   (C)   (D)

9. Give the package to whomever has the authority to sign for it.
                       (A)   (B)   (C) (D)

10. When he visited the doctor, the doctor told John that he should gone to the hospital immediately.
                (A)   (B)   (C)   (D)

11. Robert often wishes he was better prepared for his exams, but he will probably never change his
                   (A)   (B)   (C)
    poor study habits.
    (D)

12. This refrigerator is very old to keep things at a proper temperature.
                        (A)   (B)   (C)   (D)

13. The meeting was so length that many people had to leave before it concluded.
    _____(A)_____   _____(B)_____   _____(C)_____   (D)

14. John was quick to inform us that his friend Vicky was most popular, intelligent girl in his class.
            _(A)_ _(B)_ (C)   _(D)_

15. The director of the program advised the students to avoid to waste time reading material that
                                 _(A)_   _(B)_   _(C)_
    was so out-of-date.
        (D)

16. There was not enough time to completely fill out the form before the bell rang.
                   _(A)_   _(B)_   (C)   _(D)_

17. Margie and Mary must have ate some bad food in the restaurant because they were very ill shortly
                    _(A)_ _(B)_   _(C)_   _(D)_
    after they left.

18. The children were surprised when the teacher had them to close their books unexpectedly.
                     _(A)_   _(B)_   _(C)_   _(D)_

19. Do you think you could lend me good pair of gloves to wear to the wedding?
                        _(A)_   _(B)_   (C) (D)

20. His speech was a careful worded attempt to evade his responsibility in the matter.
                      _(A)_   _(B)_   _(C)_   (D)

21. The Joneses have visited Hawaii and Alaska, and they assure me that they like Alaska the best.
               _(A)_   _(B)_   _(C)_   _(D)_

22. We must have a exact count of the number of people expected to attend the closing ceremonies.
       _(A)_ (B)   _(C)_   _(D)_

23. The stage production that we saw in New York was very much as the one we had previously seen
        (A)   _(B)_   _(C)_   _____(D)_____
    in London.

24. Did you hear many news about the political situation while you were in that country?
                 _(A)_   _(B)_   _(C)_   (D)

25. Both John, Bob and Tom are outstanding golfers and reasonably good tennis players.
     (A)   _(B)_   _(C)_   (D)

26. Kathy was definitely a faster swimmer than anyone on her team and appeared headed for the state
                          _(A)_   _(B)_ (C)   _(D)_
    championship.

GO ON TO THE NEXT PAGE

27. The article suggests that when a person is under unusual stress you should be especially careful to
    (A)   (B)   (C)
    eat a well-balanced diet.
        (D)

28. Economics, with their widespread range of practical application, is of great interest to government
    (A)   (B)   (C)
    leaders throughout the world.
            (D)

29. The Tyrrels had such warm welcome from their family that they were overwhelmed and
                        (A)   (B)
    could not speak for a few minutes.
        (C)   (D)

30. Even though he was exhausted, John wrote to his parents a letter explaining the situation.
        (A)   (B)   (C)   (D)

31. Since I have so many letters to write, I am going to buy several boxes of stationary.
        (A)   (B)   (C)   (D)

32. Our friends got a bank loan for to buy a new car.
               (A)   (B)   (C)   (D)

33. By the time Robert will finish writing the first draft of his paper, most of the other students will
                        (A)   (B)   (C)
    be completing their final draft.
        (D)

34. Some members of the committee were opposed to use the club members' money to redecorate the
                                            (A)   (B)   (C)
    meeting hall.
        (D)

35. I was very shocked to see how much my grandmother she had aged since the last time we visited.
                (A)   (B)   (C)   (D)

36. Our supervisor finally noticed that it was we, Diana and me, who always turned in our reports on
                                            (A) (B)   (C)   (D)
    time.

37. In our opinion that girl is enough beautiful to be a movie star.
    (A)   (B)   (C)   (D)

38. The report that Karl wrote on the mating behavior of the bees in this area was definitely better
                            (A)   (B)   (C)
    than Bob.
        (D)

39. We were pleased to have the opportunity to watch such talented dancers to perform a highly
                                                        (A)   (B)   (C) (D)
    acclaimed new ballet.

40. The flag <u>is risen</u> at 6:30 <u>every</u> <u>morning</u> <u>without fail.</u>
        (A) (B)   (C)   (D)

41. When the Claybornes bought their new home, they painted <u>every</u> room, <u>laid</u> carpet in the living
                                                                                        (A)   (B)

room and hall, and <u>had refinished</u> the <u>kitchen</u> cabinets.
                          (C)   (D)

42. That student from Mexico <u>who</u> is <u>rooming</u> with Bill Smith reminds <u>me</u> <u>to</u> my uncle.
                                      (A)   (B)   (C)(D)

43. When <u>they</u> travel to Europe, the Harrises like to stay in Paris and <u>visiting</u> as <u>many</u> art <u>galleries</u> as
             (A)   (B)   (C)   (D)
possible.

44. She <u>never</u> is <u>diligent</u> <u>about</u> <u>practicing</u> the piano.
             (A)   (B)   (C)   (D)

45. <u>During</u> that terrible snowstorm, the police <u>demanded</u> that people <u>stayed</u> off Highway 101 <u>except</u>
        (A)   (B)   (C)   (D)
in cases of emergency.

46. He <u>refused</u> <u>to tell</u> us <u>why</u> <u>was he</u> crying.
            (A)   (B) (C)   (D)

47. Please <u>be sure</u> that everybody has <u>their</u> ticket ready <u>to give</u> to the man at the <u>door.</u>
               (A)   (B)   (C)   (D)

48. We believe that he already feels very <u>badly</u> about his mistake and we <u>have decided</u> to take <u>no</u>
                                              (A)   (B)   (C)
<u>further</u> action.
  (D)

49. <u>They</u> <u>who</u> are willing to <u>spend</u> the necessary time will find this workshop to be a <u>rewarding</u>
        (A)   (B)   (C)   (D)
experience.

50. Please see if you can <u>repair</u> the <u>door's</u> <u>knob</u> <u>before</u> Saturday morning.
                             (A)   (B)   (C)   (D)

51. The passenger <u>only</u> had a five-dollar <u>bill</u> <u>with</u> him <u>when</u> he boarded the bus.
                       (A)   (B) (C)   (D)

52. It is <u>not longer</u> necessary <u>for</u> all employees to wear an <u>identification badge</u> <u>in order</u> to work in the
             (A)   (B)   (C)   (D)
vault.

GO ON TO THE NEXT PAGE

53. In the chapter one of that book there is a really good explanation of photosynthesis, complete with
    (A)   (B)   (C)   (D)
    illustrations.

54. The salesman told me that a good set of tires were supposed to last at least twenty thousandmiles.
                                   (A)   (B)   (C)   (D)

55. Sitting under an umbrella at a tiny table in a sidewalk cafe, Bob was startled when a gust of wind
    (A)   (B)
    suddenly carried it away.
    (C)   (D)

Sentence Completion

Directions: In the Sentence Completion questions, one or more words are left out of each sentence. Under each sentence, you will see four words or phrases. Select the one word or phrase that completes the sentence correctly, then write it in the space provided in the book or on a separate sheet of paper.

56. Riding my bicycle home from school, _____ as I went around the corner.

    (A) a car hit me
    (B) I was striked by a car
    (C) I was struck by a car
    (D) I was struck with a car

57. Doctor Martin is the kind of doctor _____ will take pains to be thorough.

    (A) which
    (B) who
    (C) whom
    (D) what

58. The two doctors received an award of several thousand dollars _____.

    (A) to be divided equally between them
    (B) which was supposed to be divided in an equal way between them
    (C) to be divided equally among them
    (D) which was to be divided between them in such a way that they would each receive an equal share

59. _____, he was able to answer all the questions on the examination.

    (A) Reading all the required material
    (B) Having reading all the required material
    (C) Having read all the required material
    (D) As it was the case that he had read all the required material

60. Exhausted, we went directly to bed and _____.

    (A) ignored him knocking on our door
    (B) ignored his knocking on our door
    (C) his knocking on our door was ignored by us
    (D) ignored his knocking with our door

61. John does not swim _____.

    (A) as fastly as Fred
    (B) as fast than Fred
    (C) as fast as Fred
    (D) as fast like Fred

62. Shakespeare wrote many plays, but in my opinion *The Merchant of Venice* was _____.

(A) the better
(B) the best
(C) the goodest
(D) the most good

63. _____ that the president's economic policy will help curb inflation.

(A) The hope
(B) It is hoped
(C) Hoping
(D) To hope

64. _____ your helpful suggestions, we are sending you a copy of our latest book.

(A) In consideration of
(B) For consideration of
(C) With consideration for
(D) In consideration with

65. John studied accounting _____ while he was at Yale.

(A) and also pursued economics
(B) and economics
(C) and he also studied economics
(D) and economics was also studied by him

Check your answers using the error key beginning on page 14.

ERROR KEY

Error Identificaion

(A) 1. (*Beauty*). See Chapter 7, "Style"—*Parts of Speech*, page 144.

(C) 2. (*this* kind). See Chapter 3, "Modifiers"—*Demonstratives*, page 27.

(D) 3. (three-*week*-old). See Chapter 3, "Modifiers"—*Hyphenated or Compound Adjectives*, page 26.

(B) 4. (in search *of*). See Chapter 7, "Style"—*Prepositions in Combinations*, page 46.

(A) 5. (*dreamed that*). See Chapter 7, "Style"—*Wordiness*, page 120.

(B) 6. (If it *rains*). See Chapter 4, "Verbs"—*Conditionals*, page 60.

(B) 7. (familiar *with*). See Chapter 7, "Style"—*Prepositions in Combinations*, page 46.

(A) 8. (sort *of man*). See Chapter 7, "Style"—*Substandard*, page 122.

(A) 9. (to *whoever* has). Chapter 5, "Pronouns"—See *Who/Whom*, page 83.

(C) 10. (should *go*). Chapter 4, "Verbs"—See *Modals*, page 62.

(B) 11. (*were* better prepared). See Chapter 4, "Verbs"—*Wishes*, page 59.

(A) 12. (*too* old). See Chapter 3, "Modifiers"—*Too, Very*, and *Enough*, page 41.

(A) 13. (so *long* that). See Chapter 3, "Modifiers"—*Cause and Result*, page 37.

(D) 14. (*the* most popular). See Chapter 3, "Modifiers"—*Superlatives*, page 35.

(B) 15. (to avoid *wasting*). See Chapter 4, "Verbs"—*Verbals*, page 64.

(B) 16. (*fill out completely*). See Chapter 3, "Modifiers"—*Split Infinitives*, page 18.

(B) 17. (must have *eaten*). See Chapter 4, "Verbs"—*Past Participles*, page 68.

(C) 18. (had them *close*). See Chapter 4, "Verbs"—*Verbals*, page 64.

(B) 19. (*a* good pair). See Chapter 3, "Articles"—*Articles*, page 39.

(A) 20. (*carefully worded*). See Chapter 3, "Modifiers"—*Adjective/Adverb Confusion*, page 21.

(D) 21. (Alaska *better*). See Chapter 3, "Modifiers"—*Comparatives*, page 33.

(B) 22. (*an* exact count). See Chapter 3, "Modifiers"—*Articles*, page 39.

(C) 23. (much *like* the one). See Chapter 3, "Modifiers"—*Sameness and Similarity*, page 31.

(A) 24. (*much* news). See Chapter 3, "Modifiers"—*Few, Little, Much* and *Many*, page 28.

(A) 25. (*John, Bob, and Tom*). See Chapter 7, "Style"—*Correlative Conjunctions*, page 139.

(C) 26. (anyone *else*). See Chapter 3, "Modifiers"—*Comparatives*, page 33.

(B) 27. (*he or she* should be). See Chapter 5, "Pronouns"—*Person*, page 88.

(B) 28. (with *its* widespread). Chapter 5, "Pronouns"—See *Number*, page 89.

(A) 29. (such *a* warm welcome). Chapter 3, "Modifiers"—See *Cause and Result*, page 37.

(B) 30. (*wrote a letter to his parents*) OR (*wrote his parents a letter*). See Chapter 6, "Basic Patterns"—*Indirect Objects*, page 99.

(D) 31. (*stationery*). See Chapter 7, "Style"—*Words Often Confused, Group III*, page 137.

(C) 32. (loan *to buy*) OR (loan *for a new car*). See Chapter 6, "Basic Patterns"—*To/For(Purpose)*, page 105.

(A) 33. (Robert *finishes*). See Chapter 4, "Verbs"—*Time Clauses*, page 56.

(B) 34. (opposed to *using*). See Chapter 4, "Verbs"—*Verbals*, page 64.

(C) 35. (*grandmother had aged*). See Chapter 6, "Basic Patterns"—*Double Subjects*, page 106.

_(C)_ **36.** (Diana and *I*). See Chapter 5, "Pronouns"—*Personal Pronouns—Case*, page 80.

_(B)_ **37.** (*beautiful enough*). See Chapter 3, "Modifiers"—*Too, Very, and Enough*, page 41.

_(D)_ **38.** (better than *Bob's*). See Chapter 3, "Modifiers"—*Comparatives*, page 33.

_(B)_ **39.** (*perform* OR *performing*). See Chapter 4, "Verbs"—*Verbals*, page 64.

_(A)_ **40.** (is *raised*). See Chapter 7, "Style"—*Usage*, page 125.

_(C)_ **41.** (and *refinished*). See Chapter 4, "Verbs"—*Tense*, page 55. See also Chapter 7, "Style"—*Parallelism*, page 117.

_(D)_ **42.** (reminds me *of*). See Chapter 7, "Style"—*Prepositions in Combinations*, page 46.

_(B)_ **43.** (*to visit*). See Chapter 7, "Style"—*Parallelism*, page 117.

_(A)_ **44.** (*is never*). See Chapter 6, "Basic Patterns"—*Order of Adverbs*, page 100.

_(C)_ **45.** (*stay off*). See Chapter 4, "Verbs"—*Verbs of "Demand,"* page 57.

_(D)_ **46.** (why *he was*). See Chapter 6, "Basic Patterns"—*Embedded Questions*, page 103.

_(B)_ **47.** (*his* ticket). See Chapter 5, "Pronouns"—*Number*, page 89.

_(A)_ **48.** (feels very *bad*). See Chapter 3, "Modifiers"—*Adjectives after Verbs of Sensation*, page 23.

_(A)_ **49.** (*Those* who are). See Chapter 5, "Pronouns"—*Those Modified*, page 92.

_(C)_ **50.** (*door* knob). See Chapter 3, "Modifiers"—*Noun Adjectives*, page 24.

_(A)_ **51.** (had *only* a five-dollar bill). See Chapter 3, "Modifiers"—*Adverbs Like* Only, page 17.

_(A)_ **52.** (*no* longer). See Chapter 3, "Modifiers"—*Negation*, page 43.

_(A)_ **53.** (In chapter *one*). See Chapter 3, "Modifiers"—*Cardinal and Ordinal Numbers*, page 30.

_(B)_ **54.** (*was* supposed). See Chapter 7, "Style"—*Subject/Verb Agreement*, page 141.

_(D)_ **55.** (*the umbrella* OR *the table*). See Chapter 5, "Pronouns"—*Faulty Reference*, page 86.

Sentence Completion

_(C)_ **56.** (A) See Chapter 3, "Modifiers"—*Dangling Modifiers*, page 19.
(B) See Chapter 4, "Verbs"—*Past Participles*, page 68.
(C) **Correct**
(D) See Chapter 7, "Style"—*Prepositions (General Use)*, page 146.

_(B)_ **57.** (A) See Chapter 5, "Pronouns"—*Relative Pronouns*, page 79.
(B) **Correct**
(C) See Chapter 5, "Pronouns"—*Who/Whom*, page 83.
(D) See Chapter 5, "Pronouns"—*Relative Pronouns*, page 79.

_(A)_ **58.** (A) **Correct**
(B) See Chapter 7, "Style"—*Wordiness*, page 120.
(C) See Chapter 7, "Style"—*Usage*, page 125.
(D) See Chapter 7, "Style"—*Wordiness*, page 120.

_(C)_ **59.** (A) See Chapter 4, "Verbs"—*Present and Perfect Participles and Infinitives*, page 71.
(B) See Chapter 4, "Verbs"—*Past Participles*, page 68.
(C) **Correct**
(D) See Chapter 7, "Style"—*Wordiness*, page 120.

_(B)_ **60.** (A) See Chapter 5, "Pronouns"—*Possessives*, page 85.
(B) **Correct**
(C) See Chapter 7, "Style"—*Voice*, page 115.
(D) See Chapter 7, "Style"—*Prepositions (General Use)*, page 146.

__(C)__ **61.** (A) See Chapter 3, "Modifiers"—
Adjective/Adverb Confusion,
page 21.

(B) See Chapter 3, "Modifiers"—
Sameness and Similarity, page 31.

(C) Correct

(D) See Chapter 3, "Modifiers"—
Sameness and Similarity, page 31.

__(B)__ **62.** (A) See Chapter 3, "Modifiers"—
Superlatives, page 35.

(B) Correct

(C) See Chapter 3, "Modifiers"—
Superlatives, page 35.

(D) See Chapter 3, "Modifiers"—
Superlatives, page 35.

__(B)__ **63.** (A) See Chapter 6, "Basic Patterns"—
Clauses, page 107.

(B) Correct

(C) See Chapter 6, "Basic Patterns"—
Clauses, page 107.

(D) See Chapter 6, "Basic Patterns"—
Clauses, page 107.

__(A)__ **64.** (A) **Correct**

(B) See Chapter 7, "Style"—*Prepositions in Combinations,* page 146.

(C) See Chapter 7, "Style"—*Prepositions in Combinations,* page 146.

(D) See Chapter 7, "Style"—*Prepositions in Combinations,* page 146.

__(B)__ **65.** (A) See Chapter 7, "Style"—*Wordiness,* page 120.

(B) Correct

(C) See Chapter 7, "Style"—*Wordiness,* page 120.

(D) See Chapter 7, "Style"—*Wordiness,* page 120. See also Chapter 7, "Style"—*Voice,* page 115.

Modifiers

3

This chapter deals with words that are modifiers—that is, they modify other words in a sentence.

Adverbs Like *Only*

Adverbs such as *only* should be placed as close as possible to the adjectives, verbs, or other adverbs they modify.

ADV. ADJ.
She has *only three* dollars.

ADV. VERB
He *only* saw her; he did not speak to her.

ADV. ADV.
Only downstairs can one find a real bargain.

Note   Some other adverbs are—*just, nearly, hardly, almost,* and *scarcely*.

Error Examples

WRONG: We only have four hours to finish this paper.
RIGHT: We have *only* four hours to finish this paper.

WRONG: She just wants to take one class.
RIGHT: She wants to take *just* one class.

WRONG: That house nearly costs sixty thousand dollars.
RIGHT: That house costs *nearly* sixty thousand dollars.

WRONG: She was so quiet that hardly he noticed her.
RIGHT: She was so quiet that he *hardly* noticed her.

WRONG: They almost drove six hundred miles.
RIGHT: They drove *almost* six hundred miles.

Exercise

> **Directions:** Write a "C" on the line if the sentence is correct. Write an "X" on the line if the adverb is not placed as closely as possible to the word it modifies.

_____ 1. If you go to window five, you will have to wait only five minutes.

_____ 2. You can use these machines only between 9 a.m. and 5 p.m.

_____ 3. He hardly knows any English.

_____ 4. That shirt almost cost twenty dollars.

_____ 5. Just ten people will be able to go today.

_____ 6. You hardly have enough time to do the first exercise.

_____ 7. We had to wait nearly ten minutes for the movie to begin.

_____ 8. She scarcely slept five hours last night.

_____ 9. We want to borrow only ten dollars.

_____ 10. The soldiers only killed one person during the battle.

Check your answers using the error key on page 49.

Split Infinitives

The *infinitive* is *to* + the simple form of the verb (*V*). Do not put an adverb between *to* and *V*.

          TO + V   ADV.
He refused to *fill out* the form *completely*.

            TO + V   ADV.
They have decided to *repeat* the directions *carefully*.

         TO + V   ADV.
We hope to *inform* him *quickly*

Error Examples

WRONG: He wanted to carefully read the directions.
  RIGHT: He wanted to *read* the directions *carefully*.

WRONG: To thoroughly understand the subject, ask an expert.
  RIGHT: *To understand* the subject *thoroughly*, ask an expert.

WRONG: He was looking for a way to rapidly complete the job.
  RIGHT: He was looking for a way *to complete* the job *rapidly*.

Exercise

Directions: Write a "C" on the line if the sentence is correct. Write an "X" on the line if any word comes between *to* and the simple form of the verb.

_____ **1.** We decided to leave the area quickly.

_____ **2.** He seemed to easily understand the situation.

_____ **3.** To really make him happy would be impossible.

_____ **4.** She used a scale to accurately weigh the vegetables.

_____ **5.** Do not try to completely finish your homework before dinner.

_____ **6.** To hastily read the material is not enough for good comprehension.

_____ **7.** He began to chatter about the event excitedly.

_____ **8.** Please try to entirely revise your work before you leave.

_____ **9.** The teacher wanted to know positively whether or not the students could come to the picnic.

_____ **10.** Bob is going to soon decide on his future course of study.

Check your answers using the error key on page 49.

Dangling Modifiers

The subject of the main clause must be the same as the understood subject of the introductory phrase. In other words, the introductory phrase modifies the subject of the main clause.

INTRODUCTORY PHRASE   MAIN CLAUSE
Looking at his watch, Mr. Jones got up and left.
                         SUBJECT

Who looked at his watch?   *Mr. Jones*

Who got up and left?   *Mr. Jones*

INTRODUCTORY PHRASE   MAIN CLAUSE
Compared to his father, John is a tall man.
                         SUBJECT

Who is compared to his father?   *John*

Who is a tall man?   *John*

INTRODUCTORY PHRASE   MAIN CLAUSE

To make a collect phone call, <u>Mary</u> *must speak to the operator.*
                          SUBJECT

    Who is making a collect phone call?   *Mary*

    Who must speak to the operator?   *Mary*

INTRODUCTORY PHRASE   MAIN CLAUSE

While a dancer in New York, <u>Kathy</u> *injured her leg.*
                          SUBJECT

    Who was a dancer in New York?   *Kathy*

    Who injured her leg?   *Kathy*

Error Examples

WRONG: Running home from school, a dog bit me.
  RIGHT: *Running home from school,* I was bitten by a dog.

WRONG: When only a child, my father took me to the circus.
  RIGHT: *When only a child,* I was taken to the circus by my father.

WRONG: Hidden in his pocket, George left the room with the key.
  RIGHT: *Having hidden the key in his pocket,* George left the room.

WRONG: To understand the directions, they must be read carefully.
  RIGHT: *To understand the directions, one* must read them carefully.

Exercise

Directions: Write a "C" on the line if the sentence is correct. Write an "X" on the line if there is a dangling-modifier error.

_____   **1.** Playing in the street, the truck hit the child.

_____   **2.** By painting and repairing as needed, your home can be kept in good condition.

_____   **3.** Before leaving, Jane kissed me goodbye.

_____   **4.** Addressed and stamped, I dropped the letter in the slot.

_____   **5.** While a student at college, my mother met my father.

_____   **6.** Walking toward the church, the stained-glass windows looked beautiful.

_____   **7.** To understand the subject, a great deal of studying must be done.

_____   **8.** Skiing down the steep hill, my heart beat crazily.

_____   **9.** Watching her daughter play, Mary thought about life as a mother.

_____   **10.** Once learned, a language cannot easily be forgotten.

_____ **11.** When only a child, my father taught me how to play soccer.

_____ **12.** Studying and reading, the day passed quickly.

_____ **13.** To make a good cup of coffee, one must begin with high-quality coffee beans.

_____ **14.** Sitting alone in his room, the strange noise frightened him.

_____ **15.** Wrapped in pretty, green paper, Phyllis put the package on the table.

Check your answers using the error key on page 49.

Adjective/Adverb Confusion

1. *Adjectives* modify nouns (N) and pronouns.

   ADJ.   N   ADJ.   N
   His *recent accident* caused a *sudden change* in his behavior.

   PRON.   ADJ.
   He is *intelligent*.

2. *Adverbs* modify verbs (V).

   VERB   ADV.   VERB   ADV.
   He *had* an accident *recently*, and his behavior *changed suddenly*.

   VERB   ADV.
   He *spoke intelligently*.

3. Adverbs also modify adjectives.

   ADV.   ADJ.
   He grew an *especially small* tree.

   ADV.   ADJ.
   He was a *highly motivated* young man.

   ADV.   ADJ.
   It was a *cleverly planned* operation.

4. Adverbs also modify other adverbs.

   ADV.   ADJ.
   She could run *very quickly*.

Notes   a. Most adverbs end in *-ly*.

       b. Some words have the same form for the adjective and adverb:

Adjective	*Adverb*
late	late
fast	fast
hard	hard

         (Do not add *-ly* to these words.)

       c. The adverb for the adjective *good* is *well*.

Error Examples

WRONG: Do it carefully, if not perfect.
  RIGHT: Do it carefully, if not *perfectly*.

WRONG: He is an extreme pleasant person.
  RIGHT: He is an *extremely* pleasant person.

WRONG: It was an interesting designed museum.
  RIGHT: It was an *interestingly* designed museum.

WRONG: He worked hardly at the factory all day.
  RIGHT: He worked *hard* at the factory all day.

WRONG: You should order that book real soon.
  RIGHT: You should order that book *really* soon.

WRONG: My sister plays the piano very good.
  RIGHT: My sister plays the piano very *well*.

Exercise

Directions: Write a "C" on the line if the sentence is correct. Write an "X" on the line if there is an adjective or adverb error.

_____ **1.** The bus arrived lately, so I missed my first class.

_____ **2.** We did not pass the test, but we certainly tried hard.

_____ **3.** The train left at exactly 5:00 p.m.

_____ **4.** When Ms. Smith went to Germany, she bought an exquisitely carved vase.

_____ **5.** They had a real good chance of winning the national competition.

_____ **6.** Computers process data efficiently.

_____ **7.** We worked hard and saved enough money to take a trip.

_____ **8.** There was a hasty called meeting to discuss the bus strike.

_____ **9.** He was thorough interested in the subject.

_____ **10.** That dress fits her perfectly.

_____ **11.** She likes her students to arrive prompt for class.

_____ **12.** We studied really hard for the test.

_____ **13.** He was bright and attractive.

_____ **14.** The child ran fastly to get to school.

_____ **15.** He wrote his paper really good.

_____ **16.** The careful organized tour of the city was a huge success.

_____ **17.** You cannot possibly imagine how embarrassed I was yesterday.

_____ **18.** Although he plays soccer well, he plays tennis bad.

_____ **19.** I read an interestingly written report.

_____ **20.** The time went by very fastly on our vacation.

Check your answers using the error key on page 49.

Adjectives after Verbs of Sensation

The following verbs of sensation are generally followed by _adjectives*_, not by adverbs: _feel, look, seem, appear, taste, smell,_ and _sound._

> VERB ADJ.
> He _feels bad._

> VERB ADJ.
> The soup _smells delicious._

> VERB ADJ.
> She _looked nervous_ before the test.

Error Examples

WRONG: Those flowers smell sweetly.
 RIGHT: Those flowers smell _sweet._

WRONG: That loud music sounds badly to me.
 RIGHT: That loud music sounds _bad_ to me.

WRONG: He looks handsomely in black.
 RIGHT: He looks _handsome_ in black.

---

* These are also called "predicate adjectives."

Exercise

> **Directions:** Write a "C" on the line if the sentence is correct. Write an "X" on the line if there is an adjective or adverb error.

_____ 1. I felt sadly when I read the letter.

_____ 2. That gossip sounds malicious.

_____ 3. The wine tastes awfully, like vinegar.

_____ 4. The girls look adorable in their party costumes.

_____ 5. Our neighbor's music sounded loudly last night.

_____ 6. Laurie seemed quiet after she read her friend's letter.

_____ 7. The roses and lilacs smell nicely every spring.

_____ 8. Do not drink that milk; it tastes sourly.

_____ 9. My sister has always looked heavy because she has broad shoulders.

_____ 10. He appeared nervously as he began to take the exam.

Check your answers using the error key on page 50.

Noun Adjectives

The first noun (N) in the following pattern is used as an adjective.

> You are all *language students*.
>
> (N above *language*, N above *students*)

Notes
    a. When nouns are used as adjectives, they do *not* have plural or possessive forms.
    b. EXCEPTIONS: The following nouns always end in *-s* but are singular in number when they are used as names of courses or sciences: *physics, mathematics, economics.*

> He is an *economics teacher*.
>
> (N above *economics*, N above *teacher*)

BUT:

> The current *economic situation* is extremely uncertain.
>
> (ADJ. above *economic*, N above *situation*)

Error Examples

WRONG: He is taking some histories classes this semester.
  RIGHT: He is taking some *history* classes this semester.

WRONG: John turned in his term's paper this morning.
  RIGHT: John turned in his *term* paper this morning.

WRONG: My friend is an economic major.
  RIGHT: My friend is an *economics* major.

Exercise

Directions: Write a "C" on the line if the sentence is correct. Write an "X" on the line if there is an error in the noun adjective.

_____ 1. Tom drove past the police's station on his way to work.

_____ 2. Joan Sutherland is my favorite opera singer.

_____ 3. I need to have my car's license renewed.

_____ 4. During the power shortage, the streets lights went out.

_____ 5. He wanted to take an economic class.

_____ 6. Many people are worried about the current world's situation.

_____ 7. The news reporter was at the scene of the accident.

_____ 8. Phyllis and Julie put up the party decorations.

_____ 9. Three footballs teams were tied for first place.

_____ 10. Mike is the new mathematics professor.

_____ 11. We need some paper napkins for the picnic.

_____ 12. The students did not like the dormitory's rules.

_____ 13. The marble floor felt like ice.

_____ 14. The television's repairman picked up my television set this morning.

_____ 15. I went to three dances recitals last year.

_____ 16. John bought some leather gloves yesterday.

_____ 17. I need to buy a plane's ticket.

_____ 18. He took many languages courses when he was in New York.

_____ 19. She put a new table lamp in her living room.

_____ 20. He is taking an advanced physic course this semester.

Check your answers using the error key on page 50.

Hyphenated or Compound Adjectives

Nouns (N) are sometimes found as part of *hyphenated* or *compound* adjectives (adjectives of more than one word joined by hyphens). These nouns are *never* plural.

HYPHENATED ADJ.
I bought a *four-hundred-year-old* painting in Hong Kong.

HYPHENATED ADJ.
The president gave a *ten-minute* speech.

Error Examples

WRONG: I lived in a two-hundred-years-old house in Rome.
 RIGHT: I lived in a two-hundred-*year*-old house in Rome.

WRONG: He bought a three-hundred-dollars suit.
 RIGHT: He bought a three-hundred-*dollar* suit.

WRONG: The teacher told us to read the five-hundred-pages book.
 RIGHT: The teacher told us to read the five-hundred-*page* book.

WRONG: I have four fifty-minutes classes every day.
 RIGHT: I have four fifty-*minute* classes every day.

WRONG: She has just bought a new four-doors Ford.
 RIGHT: She has just bought a new four-*door* Ford.

Exercise

Directions: Write a "C" on the line if the sentence is correct. Write an "X" on the line if there is an error with a hyphenated adjective.

_____   **1.** We signed up for a three-hour lab.

_____   **2.** The police suspected a thirty-years-old man.

_____   **3.** My mother bought some five-dollars-a-pound cheese.

_____   **4.** John got a ten-speed bicycle for his birthday.

_____   **5.** I visited the five-thousand-years-old pyramids in Egypt last summer.

_____   **6.** John and Sue brought me a two-ounces bottle of French perfume.

_____   **7.** My parents are going on a four-week European tour next month.

_____   **8.** Most ten-month-old babies cannot walk.

_____   **9.** They are studying the five-hundred-pages manual.

_____ **10.** The Smiths have just purchased a ten-rooms house.

Check your answers with the error key on page 50.

Demonstratives

The demonstratives *this* and *that* (singular) and *these* and *those* (plural) must agree in number with the nouns they modify.

SING. SING.
John does not like *this kind* of class.
PL. PL.
What do you think of *these kinds* of chairs?

Error Examples

WRONG: These type of potato is native to Peru.
 RIGHT: *This* type of potato is native to Peru.

WRONG: That kinds of women are likely to succeed in business.
 RIGHT: *Those* kinds of women are likely to succeed in business.

WRONG: Jane never buys these brand of canned goods.
 RIGHT: Jane never buys *this* brand of canned goods.

Exercise

> **Directions:** Write a "C" on the line if the sentence is correct. Write an "X" on the line if there is an error with the demonstrative modifiers.

_____ 1. They did not like those kinds of imported cars.

_____ 2. The farmers could not find any buyers for these class of wheat.

_____ 3. This kind of story is not suitable for young children.

_____ 4. Those kinds of books are fascinating and helpful.

_____ 5. Do you think we should buy these kind of flowers for the front yard?

_____ 6. Mary never shops in those kind of expensive specialty shops.

_____ 7. He took that news badly.

_____ 8. Bob should not have bought these pair of shoes.

_____ 9. This movies are restricted to people over 17 years of age.

_____ 10. Although Bill has owned many kinds of cars, he has never considered buying this kind before.

Check your answers using the error key on page 50.

Few, Little, Much, and *Many*

1. *Few, fewer,* and *fewest,* as well as *many,* are followed by *plural count nouns* (PL. CN).

   PL. CN
   There are *few students* from Japan in our English class.

   PL. CN
   This year we received *fewer replies* to our ad than ever before.

   PL. CN
   John has *the fewest chapters* left to read of anyone in the class.

   PL. CN
   There are *many reasons* to study hard for that test.

2. *Little, less,* and *least,* as well as *much,* are followed by *non-count nouns* (NCN).

   NCN
   He gave me a *little advice* about choosing a school.

   NCN
   Susan has *less money* than I.

   NCN
   He did *the least amount* of work of anyone in the class.

   NCN
   There is not *much time* to finish this job completely.

   Notes   a. In general, *plural count nouns* can be recognized by the *-s* plural form. However, do not forget that the following words are plural: *people, men, women, children,* and *police.*

   b. The following are examples of non-count nouns: *fruit, homework, bread, money, furniture,* and *time.* Do not add *-s* to these words.

   c. The word *news* looks plural, but it is a non-count noun. Example: Little *news* is coming from that country.

   d. For *number* and *amount* see Chapter 7 "Style" and look under *Usage* on page 125.

Error Examples

WRONG: There are much books on the shelf.
 RIGHT: There are *many* books on the shelf.

WRONG: There is not many industry in that town.
 RIGHT: There is not *much* industry in that town.

WRONG: He had few winter clothing when he arrived.
 RIGHT: He had *little* winter clothing when he arrived.

WRONG: You need a little dollars to buy this book.
 RIGHT: You need a *few* dollars to buy this book.

WRONG: Lloyd scored the least points in the basketball game.
RIGHT: Lloyd scored the *fewest* points in the basketball game.

WRONG: Isabelle bought less than ten items.
RIGHT: Isabelle bought *fewer* than ten items.

Exercise

Directions: Write a "C" on the line if the sentence is correct. Write an "X" on the line if there is an error with *many, few, much,* or *little.*

_____ 1. I do not like many sugar in my coffee.

_____ 2. They did not put much furniture in their new office.

_____ 3. We did not have much knowledge about physics.

_____ 4. Of the four people injured in the accident, the child needed the fewest medical attention.

_____ 5. John had so few news from his parents that he was worried.

_____ 6. I usually have little money at the end of the month.

_____ 7. Debby spent less time studying for the exam than Robin did.

_____ 8. He predicted that few people would die of radiation poisoning.

_____ 9. Bill has the least cavities of anyone in his class.

_____ 10. We wanted to go on vacation, but we had few money.

_____ 11. There were so few good seats left that we decided not to buy tickets to the concert.

_____ 12. Nowadays, much women are becoming lawyers.

_____ 13. That party did not have much entertainment.

_____ 14. There is not many news available on that subject.

_____ 15. During the war, our government received fewer information about the situation in that country.

_____ 16. There were a little people waiting to buy tickets.

_____ 17. He had so many homework that he could not go to the movies.

_____ 18. Although she was rich, she wore little jewelry.

_____ 19. There were so much campus police at the football game that there was no trouble.

_____ 20. He did not eat many fruit in the winter.

Check your answers using the error key on page 50.

Cardinal and Ordinal Numbers

There are two kinds of numbers, *cardinal* and *ordinal*.

Examples

Cardinal	Ordinal
one	first
two	second
three	third
four	fourth
five	fifth
six	sixth
ten	tenth
twenty-one	twenty-first

The following two patterns are used to designate items in a series:

1. Ordinal numbers are used in this pattern: ***the* + ordinal + noun (N)**

    THE + ORDINAL + N
    The first book of the series is about verbs.

2. Cardinal numbers are used in this pattern: **noun (N) + cardinal**

    N + CARDINAL
    Book One of the series is about verbs.

Notes   a. Use *the* with ordinal numbers.

b. Do not use *the* with cardinal numbers.

c. Be careful to use the correct word order for each pattern.

Error Examples

WRONG: We are supposed to read the chapter seven for homework.
RIGHT: We are supposed to read *chapter seven* for homework.

WRONG: Pick up your boarding passes at gate the fifth.
RIGHT: Pick up your boarding passes at *gate five*.

WRONG: Terminal first on your right is Pan American.
RIGHT: *The first terminal* on your right is Pan American.

WRONG: We reviewed lesson the tenth in class today.
RIGHT: We reviewed lesson *ten* in class today.

WRONG: The subway stop second is Broadway.
RIGHT: *The second* subway stop is Broadway.

Exercise

Directions: Write a "C" on the line if the sentence is correct. Write an "X" on the line if there is a number error.

_____ **1.** The first checkout stand is for cash customers only.

_____ **2.** The answer is in the line fifteen on page four.

_____ **3.** Do the exercise one in your book.

_____ **4.** Pick up your receipt at teller fourth.

_____ **5.** The car designers modified their plans for the hundredth time.

_____ **6.** Pick up your check at window the third.

_____ **7.** I met him on the second day of the fall semester.

_____ **8.** You will find the bread in aisle the first.

_____ **9.** The well-known basketball player from Chicago made the first points of the game.

_____ **10.** The instructions are on the six page.

Check your answers using the error key on page 51.

Sameness and Similarity

Sameness and similarity are expressed by the following patterns:

1. *like* or *the same as*

> Your car is *like* mine. (*similarity*)

> Your car is *the same as* mine. (*sameness*)

2. *the same* + noun + *as*

> John is *the same height* as Bill.

> Mary is *the same age* as Valerie.

3. *as* + adjective + *as*

> John is *as tall as* Bill.

> Mary is *as old as* Valerie.

Error Examples

WRONG: I would like to have an apartment as the one my friend has.
 RIGHT: I would like to have an apartment *like* the one my friend has.

WRONG: Their backyard is as beautiful like a picture.
 RIGHT: Their backyard is *as beautiful as* a picture.

WRONG: He looks as his grandmother.
 RIGHT: He looks *like* his grandmother.

WRONG: This book is the same long as that one.
 RIGHT: This book is *as long as* that one.

WRONG: John is as tall than Bob.
 RIGHT: John is *as tall as* Bob.

WRONG: Mike's eyes are the same color that mine.
 RIGHT: Mike's eyes are *the same color as* mine.

WRONG: Her job pays the same salary like mine.
 RIGHT: Her job pays *the same salary as* mine.

Exercise

Directions: Write a "C" on the line if the sentence is correct. Write an "X" on the line if the comparative pattern is incorrect.

_____ 1. I would like to go to a school as the one my sister goes to.

_____ 2. His hair is the same length as mine.

_____ 3. Your apartment is the same size to mine.

_____ 4. That garden is as beautiful like the one in the park.

_____ 5. Elizabeth is the same weight as her girlfriend.

_____ 6. Your homework is the same as mine.

_____ 7. She looks as her mother.

_____ 8. This blouse is the same expensive as that one.

_____ 9. I would like to buy some earrings like yours.

_____ 10. He is as intelligent than his brother.

_____ 11. Your sofa is almost like hers.

_____ 12. He looks like his grandfather.

_____ 13. Tom's suit is the same style that Bob's.

_____ 14. This material feels like silk.

_____ 15. Your shoes are the same color like mine.

Check your answers using the error key on page 51.

Comparatives

1. One-syllable adjectives and two-syllable adjectives ending in -y* form the comparative by adding -er.

>   ADJ.   ADJ.+ -ER
> John is *tall*, but Bill is *taller*.

>   ADJ.   ADJ.+ -ER
> Mr. Smith is *busy*, but Mr. Brown is *busier*.

2. Most two- and three-syllable adjectives form the comparative by putting *more* before the adjective.

>   ADJ.   MORE + ADJ.
> Betty is *beautiful*, but her sister is *more beautiful*.

3. Some adjectives have irregular comparatives (IRR. COMP.) and must be memorized. Examples: *good, better; bad, worse*.

>   ADJ.   IRR.COMP.
> This book is *good*, but that one is *better*.

>   ADJ.   IRR.COMP.
> This soup is *bad*, but that soup is *worse*.

4. *Than* is the *only* structure word that can follow comparatives.

>   COMP. + THAN
> Their problem is *worse than* your problem.

Notes

a. Do not use both -er and *more* in the same comparative structure.

b. Be careful to use only *than* after a comparative structure.

c. Be careful to use the comparative for two items, not three or more. For three or more, use the *superlative*. See *Superlatives* in this chapter on page 35.

Error Examples

There are two main kinds of errors with comparatives, errors in structure and errors in logic.

Structure Errors

WRONG: Betty is more smarter than her classmates.
RIGHT: Betty is *smarter* than her classmates.

WRONG: This building is more expensive as that one.
RIGHT: This building is more expensive *than* that one.

WRONG: Jane had much longer hair that her sister.
RIGHT: Jane had much longer hair *than* her sister.

WRONG: I own two cars, a Ford and a Chevrolet. I like the Chevrolet the best.
RIGHT: I own two cars, a Ford and a Chevrolet. I like the Chevrolet *better*.

---

    * Change the -y to -i before adding -er.

Logic Errors

Do not compare two nouns that cannot be compared.

WRONG: John's salary was much larger than Bob.
(*Salary* cannot be compared to *Bob*.)

  RIGHT: John's salary was much larger than *that of Bob*.

           OR

           John's salary was much larger than *Bob's*.

WRONG: The number of people at the meeting is larger than last week.
(*Number* cannot be compared to *week*.)

  RIGHT: The number of people at the meeting is larger than *that at last week's meeting*.

Do not compare a noun to itself.

WRONG: Mary is smarter than anybody in her class.
(Mary is a member of the class. Mary cannot be smarter than herself.)

  RIGHT: Mary is smarter than *any other student* in the class.

           OR

           Mary is smarter than *anybody else* in the class.

WRONG: Alaska is larger than any state in the United States.
(Alaska is one of the states in the United States. It cannot be larger than itself.)

  RIGHT: Alaska is larger than *any other state* in the United States.

Exercise

Directions: Write a "C" on the line if the sentence is correct. Write an "X" on the line if there is an error in the comparative pattern.

_____ 1. This book is more better than that one.

_____ 2. This year's prices will certainly be much higher as last year's prices.

_____ 3. Since there were two possible ways to get to New York, we had to decide which one was better.

_____ 4. The customs in his country are more traditional than those in the United States.

_____ 5. Her letter was more friendlier than his.

_____ 6. She was happier than anybody in her family.

_____ 7. Nancy was luckier than Fred in Las Vegas.

_____ 8. Betty's homework is usually more organized than that of any other student's in the class.

_____ 9. The weather was much hotter this year than 1970.

_____ 10. The final exam was more difficult than the mid-semester exam.

_____ **11.** The first performance was more crowded as the second one.

_____ **12.** The new student reads faster than anyone else in the class.

_____ **13.** Fred's project proposal was much more economical than Brad's.

_____ **14.** Robert's new home is more expensive than any house in the neighborhood.

_____ **15.** Henry had a rather bad accident, and it was a miracle that he was not hurt more worse than he was.

Check your answers using the error key on page 51.

Superlatives

Use the _superlative_ to make a comparison among three or more things.

1. One-syllable adjectives and two-syllable adjectives ending in -_y_ form the superlative by adding -_est_. Always use _the_ in the superlative pattern.

   > THE + ADJ. + -EST
   > Bill is taller than John, but Bob is _the tallest_.

   > THE + ADJ. + -EST
   > Bill is happier than John, but Bob is _the happiest_.

2. Two- and three-syllable adjectives form the superlative by putting _the most_ before the adjective.

   > THE MOST + ADJ.
   > Susan is more beautiful than Betty, but Jane is _the most beautiful_ .

3. Some adjectives have irregular superlatives (IRR. SUPRL.) that must be memorized. For example: _good_, _the best_; _bad_, _the worst_.

   > THE + IRR. SUPRL.
   > Your book is better than his book, but our book is _the best_.

   > THE + IRR. SUPRL.
   > Your problem is worse than mine, but his problem is _the worst_ .

Notes   a. Always use _the_ in the superlative pattern.

b. Be careful not to use -_est_ and _most_ in the same superlative pattern.

c. Do not put _than_ after the superlative.

d. Be careful to use the superlative for three or more items. Use the comparative for two items. See _Comparatives_ on page 33 of this chapter.

Error Examples

WRONG: Yesterday was coldest day of the year.
 RIGHT: Yesterday was *the* coldest day of the year.

WRONG: John is the smartest student than anyone else in the class.
 RIGHT: John is the smartest student *in the class*.

WRONG: We went to Ann's Restaurant, Ted's Diner, and Tom's Cafe, and Ann's Restaurant served better food.
 RIGHT: We went to Ann's Restaurant, Ted's Diner, and Tom's Cafe, and Ann's Restaurant served *the best* food.

WRONG: I took mathematics, French, and history last semester, and the mathematics course was the better.
 RIGHT: I took mathematics, French, and history last semester, and the mathematics course was *the best*.

WRONG: She was the most beautifulest woman I had ever seen.
 RIGHT: She was the *most beautiful* woman I had ever seen.

Exercise

Directions: Write a "C" on the line if the sentence is correct. Write an "X" on the line if there is an error in the superlative pattern.

_____ **1.** They were the most poorest people I had ever seen.

_____ **2.** Germany is one of the most highly industrialized nations in the world.

_____ **3.** When he won the contest, he was the most surprised person than the other contestants.

_____ **4.** I went to Belgium, Holland, and England last year, and I liked Belgium better.

_____ **5.** Is the Sahara the largest desert in the world?

_____ **6.** August is hottest and most humid month of the year.

_____ **7.** It was the most biggest building I had ever seen.

_____ **8.** That company sold the most sophisticated computer equipment that we had ever found.

_____ **9.** Dr. Henderson was the most thorough doctor than Jane had ever known.

_____ **10.** John, Phyllis, and Mary were all saving money to go to Egypt, and John saved the most.

_____ **11.** Paula, Susie, and Jill bought new homes, but Paula's was more elegant.

_____ **12.** Peking is most densely populated city in the world.

_____ **13.** The damage caused by the hurricane was the worst than had ever occurred in that state.

_____ **14.** She bought a new color television, a stereo unit, and an AM/FM radio, and the television was the most expensive.

_____ **15.** Mary is the fastest runner than the other team members.

_____ **16.** You can use any of these three pens, but the red one is the best for marking on heavy material.

_____ **17.** That place serves the goodest ice cream in town.

_____ **18.** Dr. Jones was certainly among the smartest men I had ever known.

_____ **19.** He got the baddest grade he had ever received on an exam.

_____ **20.** The crimes committed by that murderer were the most heinous in the history of that town.

Check your answers using the error key on page 51.

Cause and Result

Cause-and-result clauses are expressed by the following patterns:

1. *So*

■ *so* + **adjective** + *that*

          ADJ.
He was *so tired that* he fell asleep.

■ *so* + **adverb** + *that*

          ADV.
He reads *so slowly that* he can never finish his homework.

■ **so* + *many* or *few* + **count noun** + *that*

She had *so many problems that* she could not concentrate.
          CN
There were *so few tickets* sold *that* the concert was cancelled.

■ **so* + *much* or *little* + **non-count noun** + *that*

          NCN
The storm caused *so much damage that* the people were forced to leave their homes.
          NCN
They had *so little interest* in the project *that* it failed.

2. *Such*

■ *such* + **adjective** + **plural count noun** + *that*

          ADJ.   PL. CN
They were *such good students that* they did very well on the TOEFL test.

■ *such* + **adjective** + **non-count noun** + *that*

          ADJ. NCN
It was *such good cake that* we asked for more.

---

    * For problems with *many* and *much*, see *Few, Little, Much,* and *Many* on page 28 of this chapter.

3. *So* or *such* (singular count nouns can use either of the following patterns)

■ **so + adjective + *a* + singular count noun +** *that*

SING. CN
He had *so bad a headache that* he left early.

■ **such + *a* + adjective + singular count noun +** *that*

SING. CN
He had *such a bad headache* that he left early.

Notes   a. Be careful not to omit *a* before a singular count noun.

b. The pattern of cause-and-result is expressed by *so/such . . . that*. Do *not* use *too* or *as*.

Error Examples

WRONG: The doctor had too many patients that he could not see them all.
RIGHT: The doctor had *so* many patients that he could not see them all.

WRONG: It was so good game that the stadium was packed.
RIGHT: It was *such a good* game that the stadium was packed.

OR

It was *so good a* game that the stadium was packed.

WRONG: The book was as interesting that I could not put it down.
RIGHT: The book was *so* interesting that I could not put it down.

WRONG: He is so shy as he never speaks in class.
RIGHT: He is so shy *that* he never speaks in class.

WRONG: They had a such good time in Rome that they always dreamed of going back.
RIGHT: They had *such* a good time in Rome that they always dreamed of going back.

WRONG: He gave me so good advice that I was very grateful to him.
RIGHT: He gave me *such* good advice that I was very grateful to him.

Exercise

Directions: Write a "C" on the line if the sentence is correct. Write an "X" on the line if there is an error in the cause-and-result clause.

_____ **1.** They had so a good meal at that restaurant that they wanted to go there again.

_____ **2.** They were such talented actors that their movie was a great success.

_____ **3.** The store had too few customers that it closed.

_____ **4.** It was such a long lesson that we could not finish it in one day.

_____ **5.** He was as rich that he owned four homes.

_____ **6.** He is so forgetful as he never pays his rent on time.

_____ **7.** She was such a good student that she won a scholarship.

_____ **8.** They had a such bad day that they got depressed.

_____ **9.** It was so warm weather that we went to the swimming pool.

_____ **10.** The old woman's handwriting was so faint that I could hardly read it.

_____ **11.** The stars are so far from the earth that we cannot see most of them.

_____ **12.** I had too many things to do that I could not finish them all.

_____ **13.** It was so confusing as I could not understand it.

_____ **14.** He spoke such good Arabic that he surprised everyone.

_____ **15.** The building was as large that we had difficulty finding his office.

Check your answers using the error key on page 52.

Articles

1. Use *a* or *an* with an unspecified singular count noun. Use *an* before a word that begins with a vowel or a vowel sound.

    I saw *a puppy* in the park yesterday.

    The woman asked for *an exact* count.

    He is *an honest* man.

2. Use *the* with specified singular and plural count nouns.

    The puppy I saw in the park was black and white.

    The engineers from Clearwater Company designed a new system for water purification.

3. Do *not* use an article with plural count nouns used in a general sense.

   Dogs make good pets.

   Astronauts go through rigorous training programs to prepare for space flights.

4. Do *not* use an article with non-count nouns used in a general sense.

   I do not like *seafood*.

   Honesty is the best policy.

Error Examples

WRONG: We went to the store and bought new stove.
 RIGHT: We went to the store and bought *a* new stove.

WRONG: Everyone should have a equal opportunity to get an education.
 RIGHT: Everyone should have *an* equal opportunity to get an education.

WRONG: They had an accident in new car they bought last week.
 RIGHT: They had an accident in *the* new car they bought last week.

WRONG: It is traditional to have the flowers at a wedding.
 RIGHT: It is traditional to *have flowers* at a wedding.

WRONG: The honesty is a virtue.
 RIGHT: *Honesty* is a virtue.

Exercise

Directions: Write a "C" on the line if the sentence is correct. Write an "X" on the line if there is an article mistake.

_____ **1.** John's friends had a farewell party for him last Friday.

_____ **2.** He tried hard to get good grade on the test.

_____ **3.** It is always difficult to make the decisions.

_____ **4.** When he lived in Paris he went to parties every weekend.

_____ **5.** They gave me a electric typewriter for my birthday.

_____ **6.** Paul began to think that he would never find the happiness.

_____ **7.** The old man no longer believed that money was the most important thing in life.

_____ **8.** He wanted to try on pair of jogging shoes at the shoe store.

_____ **9.** In all his life he had never wanted to try the wine.

_____ **10.** She does not have an understanding of the subject yet.

_____ **11.** I just saw boys from Africa that I met at the International House party last week.

_____ **12.** Teachers usually spend many hours correcting papers.

_____ **13.** Some people believe that the frankness is the best policy in any situation.

_____ **14.** The man who fixed my air-conditioning unit accidentally broke the fan.

_____ **15.** The doctors have to go to school for many years to complete their education.

Check your answers using the error key on page 52.

Too, Very, and *Enough*

Compare the meanings and patterns of *too*, *very*, and *enough*:

1. *Very* means *to a high degree*, but does not suggest impossibility or undesirability.

   VERY + ADJ.
   Mary is *very intelligent*.

2. *Too* suggests *impossibility* or *undesirable degree*.

   TOO + ADJ. + TO + V
   She is *too sick to come* to class today.

3. *Enough* suggests *possibility* or *sufficient degree*.

   ADJ. + ENOUGH + TO + V
   He is *tall enough to play* basketball.

Notes   a. Be careful to put *enough* AFTER the adjective.

        b. Be careful to put *to* + V (infinitive) AFTER *enough*.

        c. In patterns 2 and 3 above, do not use any other structure word after the adjective or adverb except *to*.

        d. In the above patterns adverbs can be used in the same position as adjectives. Example: Mary sings *very well*.

        e. *Enough* can come before or after a noun to express sufficiency.

           He had *money enough* to buy a new car.

                OR

           He had *enough money* to buy a new car.

Error Examples

WRONG: This meat is too delicious.
RIGHT: This meat is *very* delicious.

WRONG: It was very late to catch the plane.
RIGHT: It was *too* late to catch the plane.

WRONG: He was enough old to get a driver's license.
RIGHT: He was *old enough* to get a driver's license.

WRONG: His English was enough good as for him to pass the TOEFL.
RIGHT: His English was *good enough* for him to pass the TOEFL.

WRONG: We had very much time to finish our work.
RIGHT: We had *enough time* to finish our work.

Exercise

Directions: Write a "C" on the line if the sentence is correct. Write an "X" on the line if there is an error with *too*, *very*, or *enough*.

_____ 1. I had enough experience to get the job.

_____ 2. This soup is too good.

_____ 3. It was too late to go to the theater.

_____ 4. He is enough intelligent to do well in school.

_____ 5. Paul had very much money to buy a new motorcycle.

_____ 6. I am very disappointed in his behavior.

_____ 7. He made too many good friends when he studied abroad.

_____ 8. She spoke French well enough to be a translator.

_____ 9. He did not speak English as well enough to be understood.

_____ 10. The envelope was thin enough to slide under the door.

_____ 11. The sofa was big enough as to seat four people comfortably.

_____ 12. This paragraph is not enough good as to be acceptable.

_____ 13. His TOEFL score was high enough to be accepted.

_____ 14. She was too happy when she heard the news.

_____ 15. She was enough old to get married.

Check your answers using the error key on page 52.

Negation

1. *Not* is an adverb that negates verbs. *Not* is used in the following patterns:

   ■ **auxiliary + *not* + V + ing**

   > AUX. + NOT + V + -ING
   > He *is not going* to the party.

   > AUX. + NOT + V + -ING
   > He *is not making* any money.

   ■ **auxiliary + *not* + V**

   > AUX. + NOT + V
   > He *does not like* to study on the weekends.

   > AUX. + NOT + V
   > We *do not want* any coffee, thank you.

   ■ **auxiliary + *not* + past participle**

   > AUX. + NOT + PAST PART.
   > He *has not been* here for days.

   > AUX. + NOT + PAST PART.
   > They *have not seen* any deer.

   ■ ***modal + *not* + V**

   > MODAL + NOT + V
   > We *will not accept* your opinion.

   > MODAL + NOT + V
   > You *should not eat* too many sweets.

2. *No* is an adjective that indicates the absence of something. It modifies nouns. It is used in the following pattern:

   ■ **Verb + *no* + noun**

   > V + NO + N
   > There *is no charge* for towels at the pool.

   > V + NO + N
   > He *has no passport* .

3. *None* is a pronoun meaning *not any* or *not one*. Use *none* when the noun it replaces has been mentioned already.

   > PRON.
   > The children ate all the *cookies*. When I arrived, there were *none* left. (*none* = no cookies)

   > PRON.
   > They asked me to contribute some *money* but I had *none*. (*none* = no money)

   None may also be used in the following pattern:

   ■ ***None + of the* + noun**

   In this pattern, the noun that *none* refers to is placed after *of the*.

   > PRON. + OF THE + N
   > When I arrived, *none of the cookies* were left.

   > PRON. + OF THE + N
   > *None of the children* know how to swim.

---

* For an explanation of modals, see the section in Chapter 4, "Verbs"—Verbs of "Demand" on page 57.

4. Remember to use *any* after negative words to express the absence of quantity for plural count nouns and non-count nouns. [*Anyone, anybody, anywhere, anymore,* and *anything* can also be used in negative sentence constructions.]

> NEG.　　ANY　　NCN
> I do *not* have *any free time* today.

> NEG. ANY　PL. CN
> There were *not any students* from China this year.

> NEG.　　　　　　ANYMORE
> He does *not* go to school *anymore.*

> NEG.　　　ANYONE
> We did *not see anyone leave the building.*

5. There are some words that have negative meanings even though they do not appear to be negative, for example: *hardly, scarcely, rarely, seldom, without,* and *only.* Do not use another negative word with these words. (See notes.)

> NEG.
> He had *scarcely* enough money for the bus.

> NEG.
> They went to bed *without* dinner.

6. Negative infinitives (*to* + V) are formed by putting *not* before the infinitive (*not* + *to* + V).

> NOT + TO + V
> She said *not to talk* during the program.

> NOT + TO + V
> They told us to relax and *not to worry* .

7. Remember that *no longer* is an idiomatic negative expression of time.

> He *no longer* lives here.

> They *no longer* play golf together.

Notes　a. To express a negative idea, use only one negative word. Two negative words in one sentence make the sentence an affirmative statement, for example, "Do *not* leave *without* an umbrella." ("Be sure to take your umbrella.")

　b. Never use *not longer* when *longer* means time.

Error Examples

WRONG: He is no going on vacation this summer.
 RIGHT: He is *not* going on vacation this summer.

WRONG: There is not butter in the refrigerator.
 RIGHT: There is *no* butter in the refrigerator.

WRONG: There were none children at the playground.
 RIGHT: There were *no* children at the playground.

WRONG: We do not have no class Friday.
  RIGHT: We do not have *any* class Friday.

WRONG: They seldom do not go to the movies.
  RIGHT: They *seldom go* to the movies.

WRONG: I encourage you to do not wait for him.
  RIGHT: I encourage you *not to wait* for him.

WRONG: She said to sit quietly and to not open our books.
  RIGHT: She said to sit quietly and *not to open* our books.

WRONG: He ran out of money and could not longer continue school.
  RIGHT: He ran out of money and could *no* longer continue school.

WRONG: The children went to the movies without no money.
  RIGHT: The children went to the movies without *any* money.

WRONG: I searched all day for some new shoes, but there were none shoes I liked.
  RIGHT: I searched all day for some new shoes, but there were *none* I liked.

Exercise

> **Directions:** Write a "C" on the line if the sentence is correct. Write an "X" on the line if there is an error in negation.

_____ **1.** He could not lend me $5 because he did not have only $3.

_____ **2.** There were several of his friends at the restaurant, but none of mine came.

_____ **3.** The rules required us to form an orderly line and to do not talk.

_____ **4.** None of the shoes on sale fit me.

_____ **5.** You are no going to finish the test in time.

_____ **6.** Rarely does one see such a handsome man.

_____ **7.** He could not longer tolerate that situation.

_____ **8.** There were not cheaper beds left at that furniture store.

_____ **9.** The director told the chorus to sit down and not to whisper.

_____ **10.** By the time I arrived, there was no birthday cake left.

_____ **11.** He could not scarcely believe what I told him.

_____ **12.** That couple has none children.

_____ **13.** Do not go to the mountains without no sturdy hiking boots.

_____ **14.** We were no interested in what they were selling.

_____ **15.** No longer can the world afford to waste its natural resources.

_____ **16.** He did not have no good reason for hitting him.

_____ **17.** If I were you I would no take that course.

_____ **18.** The Smiths could afford to pay only $40,000 for a new home, and they were quite dismayed to learn that there were none available in that price range.

_____ **19.** The children could not hardly believe their eyes when they saw a giraffe for the first time.

_____ **20.** They foolishly drove into the desert without any extra water.

Check your answers using the error key on page 52.

Chapter Quiz

Error Identification

> **Directions:** For the Error Identification questions, each sentence contains four underlined words or phrases. Select the one word or phrase that must be changed in order for the sentence to be correct. Write your answer on the line or on a separate sheet of paper.

1. He found an interesting lithograph as the one he had seen on his trip to Spain.
                 (A)   (B)   (C) (D)

2. I told him as forceful as possible that he would not be allowed to enter the room without written
            (A)   (B)   (C)   (D)
permission.

3. Dr. Fields received so large bill when he checked out of the hotel that he did not have
                 (A)   (B)   (C)
enough money to pay for a taxi to the airport.
(D)

4. Although David had originally agreed to help her, he later decided it would be more
                (A)   (B)
time-consuming that he had anticipated.
(C)   (D)

5. The hunters were able to take their limit of game with few effort in spite of the unusually rainy
              (A)   (B)   (C)   (D)
weather.

6. In spite of the wonderful acting, sensitive photography, and well-developed plot, the three-hours
    (A)   (B)   (C)
movie could not hold our attention.
(D)

7. The weatherman <u>suggests</u> <u>keeping</u> small children out of the sun because he predicts <u>that</u> today will
                      (A)   (B)   (C)
    be <u>hottest</u> day of the year.
          (D)

8. The American businessmen were perplexed by the <u>much</u> considerations that the foreign company
                                                     (A)
    <u>had</u> to take <u>into</u> account before <u>arriving</u> at a decision.
     (B)   (C)   (D)

9. The new zoo, with <u>its</u> elaborate moat system and open spaces, <u>was</u> <u>enough roomy</u> to
                       (A)   (B)   (C)
    accommodate <u>even</u> very large animals comfortably.
                  (D)

10. All of the players <u>were anticipating</u> the last game of the series, <u>which</u> they expected to be <u>real</u>
                            (A)   (B)   (C) (D)
    exciting.

11. Having <u>given</u> serious consideration to a job offer from another company, Bob finally decided to
            (A)
    <u>completely</u> forget about the offer and to <u>continue</u> at <u>his</u> old job.
       (B)   (C)   (D)

12. I <u>scarcely have</u> <u>enough</u> money to <u>pay</u> the bill I <u>received</u> for medical services.
           (A)   (B)   (C)   (D)

13. After <u>having dinner</u> in that restaurant last night, I felt <u>badly</u> and my wife <u>had</u> to take me to the
            (A)   (B)   (C) (D)
    hospital.

14. <u>Before leaving</u> for her <u>two-week</u> vacation, Sharon had to <u>quickly</u> prepare the monthly <u>financial</u>
        (A)   (B)   (C)   (D)
    report.

15. A prize <u>was awarded</u> to <u>millionth</u> person <u>who</u> bought a <u>year's</u> subscription to the magazine.
                (A)   (B)   (C)   (D)

16. Although Niagara Falls in the United States is not as high <u>than</u> Angel Falls in Venezuela, more
                                                  (A)   (B)
    tourists visit Niagara Falls because <u>it</u> is more <u>accessible</u>.
                                          (C)   (D)

17. Seriously <u>burned</u> in a terrible car accident, the doctor was not sure that John <u>could be protected</u>
                (A)   (B)
    from infection <u>long enough</u> for his body to <u>begin to heal itself</u>.
                      (C)   (D)

18. My friend Dorothy, <u>who</u> just <u>got back</u> from Paris, said that the view from the top of the Eiffel
                        (A)   (B)
    Tower <u>was</u> <u>too</u> breathtaking.
           (C)   (D)

19. After a long, <u>seemingly</u> futile search, Professor Clayborne was <u>finally</u> able to locate the <u>five</u>
          (A)   (B)   (C)
    volume of the series he needed <u>to continue</u> his research.
                               (D)

20. They <u>only publish</u> stories that <u>are</u> suitable for young children <u>to read</u>.
         (A)   (B)   (C)   (D)

21. Because of the <u>long, detailed</u> questions and the <u>unfamiliar</u> format, John <u>could not scarcely</u> finish
              (A)   (B)   (C)
    the <u>test on time</u>.
         (D)

22. Clark spent <u>many</u> years <u>studying</u> Eastern philosophy in his search for the meaning of <u>the life</u>.
               (A)   (B)   (C)   (D)

23. Although he <u>had scaled</u> many of the <u>world's tallest</u> mountains, he was still <u>looking for</u> <u>more taller</u>
              (A)   (B)   (C)   (D)
    peaks to climb.

24. The mechanic <u>recently</u> purchased <u>these</u> set of tools <u>in order</u> to be able to work on <u>large</u> diesel
               (A)   (B)   (C)   (D)
    trucks.

25. We all looked forward to <u>going</u> on our <u>class's</u> picnic on the <u>last</u> day of the semester.
               (A) (B)   (C)   (D)

26. They were <u>completely</u> unprepared for the difficulties of <u>caring</u> for a <u>three-months-old</u> baby <u>on</u>
             (A)   (B)   (C)   (D)
    their European trip.

27. <u>Driving</u> across the bridge, the sailboat with its sails <u>billowing</u> in the wind <u>was</u> a beautiful sight to
     (A)   (B)   (C)   (D)
    see.

28. They could not help <u>noticing</u> the article <u>posted</u> about a <u>unusual</u> flying object seen <u>recently</u>.
                      (A) (B)   (C)   (D)

29. <u>Even though</u> my friend considered a career in economics or business administration, he <u>finally</u>
       (A)   (B)
    decided on a <u>physic</u> major.
      (C)   (D)

30. As he was driving me home, he told me <u>that</u> he <u>not longer</u> spent his winters in <u>Florida</u>.
    (A)   (B)   (C)   (D)

Check your answers using the error key beginning on page 53.

ERROR KEYS

(All references to rules and notes refer to the specific section where the quiz appears.)

Adverbs like *Only*

C 1.
C 2.
X 3. (*hardly* any English). *Hardly* modifies *any*.
X 4. (*almost* twenty dollars). *Almost* modifies *twenty*.
C 5.
X 6. (*hardly* enough time). *Hardly* modifies *enough*.
C 7.
X 8. (*scarcely* five hours). *Scarcely* modifies *five*.
C 9.
X 10. (*only* one person). *Only* modifies *one*.

Split Infinitives

C 1.
X 2. (*to understand the situation easily*)
X 3. (*To make him really happy*)
X 4. (*to weigh the vegetables accurately*)
X 5. (*to finish your homework completely*)
X 6. (*To read the material hastily*)
C 7.
X 8. (*to revise your work entirely*)
C 9.
X 10. (*to decide soon*)

Dangling Modifiers

X 1. (Playing in the street, *the child was hit by the truck.*)
X 2. (By painting and repairing as needed, *one can keep one's home in good condition.*)
C 3.
X 4. (*After I had addressed and stamped the letter, I dropped it in the slot.*)
C 5.

X 6. (*Walking toward the church, I noticed the beautiful stained-glass windows.*)
X 7. (*To understand the subject, one must do a great deal of studying.*)
X 8. (*Skiing down the steep hill, I felt my heart beat crazily.*)
C 9.
C 10.
X 11. (*When I was only a child*, my father taught me how to play soccer.)
X 12. (*Studying and reading, I passed the day quickly.*)
C 13.
X 14. (*Sitting alone in his room, he was frightened by the strange noise.*)
X 15. (*Having wrapped the package in pretty green paper, Phyllis put it on the table.*)

Adjective/Adverb Confusion

X 1. (*late*). See note b.
C 2.
C 3.
C 4. Note: In this sentence, the adverb *exquisitely* modifies the adjective *carved*; however, a similar sentence could be constructed using the adjective *exquisite* to modify the noun vase (. . . an exquisite, carved vase).
X 5. (*really* good chance). See rule 3.
C 6.
C 7.
X 8. (*hastily* called). See rule 3.
X 9. (*thoroughly* interested). See rule 3.
C 10.
X 11. (to arrive *promptly*). See rule 2.
C 12.
C 13.
X 14. (*fast*). See note b.
X 15. (really *well*). See rule 2 and note c.

_X_ **16.** (*carefully* organized). See rule 3.

_C_ **17.**

_X_ **18.** (plays tennis *badly*). See rule 2.

_C_ **19.**

_X_ **20.** (very *fast*). See note b.

Adjectives after Verbs of Sensation

_X_ **1.** (*sad*)

_C_ **2.**

_X_ **3.** (*awful*)

_C_ **4.**

_X_ **5.** (*loud*)

_C_ **6.**

_X_ **7.** (*nice*)

_X_ **8.** (*sour*)

_C_ **9.**

_X_ **10.** (*nervous*)

Noun Adjectives

_X_ **1.** (*police* station). See note a.

_C_ **2.**

_X_ **3.** (*car* license). See note a.

_X_ **4.** (*street* lights). See note a.

_X_ **5.** (an *economics* class). See note b.

_X_ **6.** (*world* situation). See note a.

_C_ **7.**

_C_ **8.**

_X_ **9.** (*football* teams). See note a.

_C_ **10.**

_C_ **11.**

_X_ **12.** (*dormitory* rules). See note a.

_C_ **13.**

_X_ **14.** (*television* repairman). See note a.

_X_ **15.** (*dance* recitals). See note a.

_C_ **16.**

_X_ **17.** (*plane* ticket). See note a.

_X_ **18.** (*language* courses). See note a.

_C_ **19.**

_X_ **20.** (*physics* course). See note b.

Hyphenated or Compound Adjectives

_C_ **1.**

_X_ **2.** (thirty-*year*-old man)

_X_ **3.** (five-*dollar*-a-pound cheese)

_C_ **4.**

_X_ **5.** (five-thousand-*year*-old pyramids)

_X_ **6.** (two-*ounce* bottle)

_C_ **7.**

_C_ **8.**

_X_ **9.** (five-hundred-*page* manual)

_X_ **10.** (ten-*room* house)

Demonstratives

_C_ **1.**

_X_ **2.** (*this* class)

_C_ **3.**

_C_ **4.**

_X_ **5.** (these *kinds*)

_X_ **6.** (those *kinds*)

_C_ **7.**

_X_ **8.** (*this* pair)

_X_ **9.** (*these* movies)

_C_ **10.**

Few, Little, Much, and *Many*

_X_ **1.** (*much* sugar). See rule 2.

_C_ **2.**

_C_ **3.**

_X_ **4.** (*least* medical attention). See rule 2.

_X_ **5.** (*little* news). See rule 2 and note c.

_C_ **6.**

_C_ **7.**

_C_ **8.**

_X_ **9.** (the *fewest* cavities). See rule 1.

_X_ **10.** (*little* money). See rule 2.

_C_ **11.**

_X_ **12.** (*many* women). See rule 1 and note a.

_C_ **13.**

_X_ **14.** (*much* news). See rule 2 and note c.

_X_ **15.** (*less* information). See rule 2.

X __ **16.** (a *few* people). See rule 1 and note a.

X __ **17.** (*much* homework). See rule 2 and note b.

C __ **18.**

X __ **19.** (*many* campus police). See rule 1 and note a.

X __ **20.** (*much* fruit). See rule 1 and note b.

Cardinal and Ordinal Numbers

C __ **1.**

X __ **2.** (in *line fifteen*). See rule 2 and note b.

X __ **3.** (Do *exercise one*). See rule 2 and note b. OR (Do *the first* exercise). See rule 1.

X __ **4.** (at teller *four*). See rule 2. OR (the *fourth* teller). See rule 1.

C __ **5.**

X __ **6.** (at *the third* window). See rule 1. OR (at *window three*). See rule 2.

C __ **7.**

X __ **8.** (in *the first* aisle). See rule 1. OR (in *aisle one*). See rule 2.

C __ **9.**

X __ **10.** (on *page six*). See rule 2.

Sameness and Similarity

X __ **1.** (*like* the one). See rule 1.

C __ **2.**

X __ **3.** (*as* mine). See rule 2.

X __ **4.** (as beautiful *as*). See rule 3.

C __ **5.**

C __ **6.**

X __ **7.** (*like* her mother). See rule 1.

X __ **8.** (the same *price* as). See rule 2. OR (*as* expensive as). See rule 3.

C __ **9.**

X __ **10.** (as intelligent *as*). See rule 3.

C __ **11.**

C __ **12.**

X __ **13.** (style *as*). See rule 2.

C __ **14.**

X __ **15.** (color *as*). See rule 2.

Comparatives

X __ **1.** (is *better* than). See note a.

X __ **2.** (higher *than*). See rule 4 and note b.

C __ **3.**

C __ **4.**

X __ **5.** (was *friendlier* than). See note a.

X __ **6.** (happier than *anybody else* in her family). See Logic Errors number 2.

C __ **7.**

C __ **8.**

X __ **9.** (much hotter this year than *that* in 1970). See Logic Errors number 1.

C __ **10.**

X __ **11.** (more crowded *than* the second one). See rule 4 and note b.

C __ **12.**

C __ **13.**

X __ **15.** (any *other* house). See Logic Errors number 2.

X __ **16.** (hurt *worse* than). See rule 3.

Superlatives

X __ **1.** (*the poorest* people). See note b.

C __ **2.**

X __ **3.** (the most surprised person *of all the contestants.*). See note c.

X __ **4.** (Belgium *the best*). See note d.

C __ **5.**

X __ **6.** (*the* hottest and *the* most humid month). See note a.

X __ **7.** (*the biggest* building). See note b.

C __ **8.**

X __ **9.** (doctor *that*). See note c.

C __ **10.**

X __ **11.** (*the most* elegant). See note d.

X __ **12.** (*the* most densely). See note a.

X __ **13.** (the worst *that*). See note c.

C __ **14.**

X __ **15.** (the fastest runner *on the team*). See note c.

C __ **16.**

_X_ **17.** (the *best* ice cream). See rule 3.

_C_ **18.**

_X_ **19.** (the *worst* grade). See rule 3.

_C_ **20.**

Cause and Result

_X_ **1.** (so good *a* meal) OR (*such* a good meal). See rule 3.

_C_ **2.**

_X_ **3.** (had *so* few customers that). See note b.

_C_ **4.**

_X_ **5.** (was *so* rich that). See note b.

_X_ **6.** (so forgetful *that*). See note b.

_C_ **7.**

_X_ **8.** (had *such* a bad day that) OR (had so bad *a* day that). See rule 3.

_X_ **9.** (was *such* warm weather that). See rule 2.

_C_ **10.**

_C_ **11.**

_X_ **12.** (had *so* many things to do that). See note b.

_X_ **13.** (so confusing *that*). See note b.

_C_ **14.**

_X_ **15.** (*so* large that). See note b.

Articles

_C_ **1.**

_X_ **2.** (*a* good grade). See rule 1.

_X_ **3.** (*to make decisions*). See rule 3.

_C_ **4.**

_X_ **5.** (*an* electric typewriter). See rule 1.

_X_ **6.** (*find happiness*). See rule 4.

_C_ **7.**

_X_ **8.** (on *a* pair of jogging shoes). See rule 1.

_X_ **9.** (*to try wine*). See rule 4.

_C_ **10.**

_X_ **11.** (saw *the* boys). See rule 2.

_C_ **12.**

_X_ **13.** (*that frankness* is). See rule 4.

_C_ **14.**

_X_ **15.** (*Doctors* have to go). See rule 3.

Too, Very, and *Enough*

_C_ **1.**

_X_ **2.** (*very* good). See rule 1.

_C_ **3.**

_X_ **4.** (*intelligent enough*). See note a.

_X_ **5.** (had *enough* money). See rule 3.

_C_ **6.**

_X_ **7.** (made *many* good friends). See rule 2.

_C_ **8.**

_X_ **9.** (English *well* enough). See rule 3 and note c.

_C_ **10.**

_X_ **11.** (big *enough to* seat). See rule 2 and note c.

_X_ **12.** (*good enough* to). See notes a and c.

_C_ **13.**

_X_ **14.** (*very* happy). See rule 1.

_X_ **15.** (*old enough*). See note a.

Negation

_X_ **1.** (he *had* only $3). See rule 5.

_C_ **2.**

_X_ **3.** (and *not to talk*). See rule 6.

_C_ **4.**

_X_ **5.** (are *not* going to). See rule 1.

_C_ **6.**

_X_ **7.** (*no* longer). See rule 7.

_X_ **8.** (*no* cheaper beds). See rule 2.

_C_ **9.**

_C_ **10.**

_X_ **11.** (*could scarcely*). See rule 5.

_X_ **12.** (*no* children). See rule 2.

_X_ **13.** (*without sturdy* hiking boots). See rule 5.

_X_ **14.** (were *not* interested). See rule 1.

_C_ **15.**

___X___   **16.** (did not have *any* good reason). See rule 4.

___X___   **17.** (would *not* take). See rule 1.

___C___   **18.**

___X___   **19.** (*could hardly* believe). See rule 5.

___C___   **20.**

Chapter Quiz

Error Identification

___(A)___   **1.** See *Sameness and Similarity*, page 31.

___(A)___   **2.** See *Adjective/Adverb Confusion*, page 21.

___(A)___   **3.** See *Cause and Result*, page 37.

___(C)___   **4.** See *Comparatives*, page 33.

___(C)___   **5.** See *Few, Little, Much,* and *Many*, page 28.

___(C)___   **6.** See *Hyphenated or Compound Adjectives*, page 26.

___(D)___   **7.** See *Superlatives*, page 35.

___(A)___   **8.** See *Few, Little, Much,* and *Many*, page 28.

___(C)___   **9.** See *Too, Very,* and *Enough*, page 41.

___(D)___   **10.** See *Adjective/Adverb Confusion*, page 23.

___(B)___   **11.** See *Split Infinitives*, page 18.

___(A)___   **12.** See *Adverbs like Only*, page 17.

___(B)___   **13.** See *Adjectives After Verbs of Sensation*, page 23.

___(C)___   **14.** See *Split Infinitives*, page 18.

___(B)___   **15.** See *Cardinal and Ordinal Numbers*, page 30.

___(B)___   **16.** See *Sameness and Similarity*, page 31.

___(A)___   **17.** See *Dangling Modifiers*, page 19.

___(D)___   **18.** See *Too, Very,* and *Enough*, page 41.

___(C)___   **19.** See *Cardinal and Ordinal Numbers*, page 30.

___(A)___   **20.** See *Adverbs like Only*, page 17.

___(C)___   **21.** See *Negation*, page 43.

___(D)___   **22.** See *Articles*, page 39.

___(D)___   **23.** See *Comparatives*, page 33.

___(B)___   **24.** See *Demonstratives*, page 27.

___(C)___   **25.** See *Noun Adjectives*, page 24.

___(C)___   **26.** See *Hyphenated or Compound Adjectives*, page 26.

___(A)___   **27.** See *Dangling Modifiers*, page 19.

___(C)___   **28.** See *Articles*, page 39.

___(D)___   **29.** See *Noun Adjectives*, page 24.

___(C)___   **30.** See *Negation*, page 43.

Verbs

4

Tense

The following are common verb-tense problems:

1. ***Present Perfect.*** Remember to use the present perfect *only* when the action has started in the past and still relates to the present.

   > I *have been* in the United States for six months.

   > She *has played* the piano since she was a child.

2. ***Past Tense.*** Remember to use the past tense when the action occurred or existed in the past.

   > I *went* to California last summer.

   > He *visited* several museums in Spain.

3. ***Past Perfect.*** Remember to use the past perfect only to express an activity that happened before another past activity.

   > The movie *had begun* when we arrived.

   > I *had* already *left* when he called.

   Notes   It is possible to use the past perfect in sentences where *before* or *after* show sequence, but it is not necessary.

Error Examples

WRONG: I have finished a game of tennis with John when Bob arrived.
 RIGHT: I *had finished* a game of tennis with John when Bob arrived.

WRONG: Since Bob graduated last year, he had been traveling around Europe.
 RIGHT: Since Bob graduated last year, he *has been traveling* around Europe.

WRONG: It has taken me a long time to do the homework last night.
 RIGHT: It *took* me a long time to do the homework last night.

WRONG: Since 1976 he is living in Brazil.
 RIGHT: Since 1976 he *has been living* in Brazil.

> OR

> Since 1976 he *has lived* in Brazil.

Exercise

> **Directions:** Write a "C" on the line if the sentence is correct. Write an "X" on the line if there is an error in the verb tense.

_____ **1.** I have been in Mexico during the summer of 1970.

_____ **2.** Mary had prepared dinner when I arrived, so we were able to eat immediately.

_____ **3.** Three years ago he had been a student at a university in California.

_____ **4.** We have collected stamps for many years.

_____ **5.** We took the bus downtown, did a few errands, and had gone to lunch.

_____ **6.** Since he bought a new car, he has been driving to work every day.

_____ **7.** Last night they have recognized us from the party we went to earlier in the week.

_____ **8.** Since Ted graduated, he has been working with his father.

_____ **9.** The doctor had seen ten patients since eight o'clock this morning.

_____ **10.** He is studying English for the last five years.

Check your answers using the error key on page 75.

Time Clauses

Use the simple present tense in future-time clauses (when the action will take place sometime in the future). (Never use *will* or *going to* in future-time clauses.) Time clauses* are introduced by such words as: *when, while, after, before, as soon as*, etc. Also see *Conditionals* in this chapter on page 60.

Future-time clauses:

$$\text{As soon as they } \underset{\text{FUTURE-TIME CL.}}{\underline{\text{get their degrees}}}^{\text{PRES}}\text{, they are going home.}$$

$$\underset{\text{FUTURE-TIME CL.}}{\underline{\text{When I } see \text{ him}}}^{\text{PRES}}\text{, I will give him your message.}$$

Error Examples

WRONG: Whenever you will be in town, call me.
 RIGHT: Whenever you *are* in town, call me.

WRONG: As soon as I will get all the vaccinations I will need, I will be leaving for Southeast Asia.
 RIGHT: As soon as I *get* all the vaccinations I need, I will be leaving for Southeast Asia.

WRONG: After Dave is going to break the track record, many universities will offer him scholarships.
 RIGHT: After Dave *breaks* the track record, many universities will offer him scholarships.

---

 * Other tenses may also be used in time clauses, but the present tense *must* be used in future-time clauses when the main clause is in the future.

Exercise

Directions: Write a "C" on the line if the sentence is correct. Write an "X" on the line if there is a mistake in the time clause.

_____ **1.** You should visit that part of the country when it will be spring.

_____ **2.** It will get cold in the desert when winter will come.

_____ **3.** As soon as you learn to swim, I will take you to our cabin at the lake.

_____ **4.** When the children are going to visit their grandmother, Henry and I will be going to Europe.

_____ **5.** When Bruce visits him tomorrow, his doctor will probably tell him to increase his medication.

_____ **6.** Will you buy me a wool jacket when you will be in Scotland?

_____ **7.** The actress who plays this role will receive an award when the critics will see her performance.

_____ **8.** When I have time, I will try to run two miles.

_____ **9.** When the fire engines go down the street, all the dogs in the neighborhood howl.

_____ **10.** As soon as Joan will get a good job, she is going to buy a condominium.

Check your answers using the error key on page 75.

Verbs of "Demand"

The simple verb (V) is used for all persons in a noun clause after the following verbs:

demand	recommend	be necessary
insist	urge	be required
require	advise	be essential
suggest	request	be important
	ask (when it means *request*)	

The doctor recommended that she *have* surgery.

I suggest that he *be* ready on time.

She asked that all employees *attend* the meeting.

Notes Use *not* to make the verb negative. Do not use *don't*.

The weatherman suggested that people *not use* Highway 7.

Error Examples

WRONG: The doctor advised that I am going on a diet.
 RIGHT: The doctor advised that I *go* on a diet.

WRONG: The restaurant suggested that we arrived on time for our reservation.
 RIGHT: The restaurant suggested that we *arrive* on time for our reservation.

WRONG: The instructions ask that we don't use a red pen.
 RIGHT: The instructions ask that we *not use* a red pen.

WRONG: The law requires that students are in school a certain number of days a year.
 RIGHT: The law requires that students *be* in school a certain number of days a year.

WRONG: It was important that money was collected for the cause.
 RIGHT: It was important that money *be* collected for the cause.

Exercise

Directions: Write a "C" on the line if the sentence is correct. Write an "X" on the line if there is an error in the verb in the noun clause after a "demand" verb.

_____ **1.** The supervisor recommended that all employees took a course in speed-reading.

_____ **2.** They request that you be fluent in Spanish.

_____ **3.** My doctor urges that I am stopping smoking immediately.

_____ **4.** It was essential that the train leave on time.

_____ **5.** The professor advised that John had a private tutor for a few weeks.

_____ **6.** The admiral demanded that his crew has inspection twice a day.

_____ **7.** They asked that she not call before 8:00 a.m.

_____ **8.** The gracious hosts insisted that Mr. Smith did not leave so early.

_____ **9.** I suggested that he wear black for the ceremony.

_____ **10.** The police require that a driver renews his license every three years.

Check your answers using the error key on page 75.

Wishes

1. *Present* wishes are expressed in the *past* tense.

> PAST
> Ralph wishes that he *had* $1,000,000. (but he doesn't)

> PAST
> Mary wishes that she *lived* in New York. (but she doesn't)

> PAST
> Grace wishes that she *did not have* a test tomorrow. (but she does)

2. Always use *were* in present wishes for *to be*.

> He has often wished that he *were* older. (but he's not)

> I often wish that I *were* in Hawaii. (but I'm not)

> We often wish that we *were not* so busy. (but we are)

> They often wish that they *were not* living in Chicago. (but they are)

3. *Past* wishes are expressed in the *past perfect*.

> PAST PERF.
> Hiromi wishes that she *had studied* more English before arriving in the United States. (but she didn't)

> PAST PERF.
> Kathy and Bob wish that they *had gotten* married before she went to Africa. (but they didn't)

> PAST PERF.
> The children wish they *had not disobeyed* their mother. (but they did)

Notes   After the verb *wish*, the noun clause may be introduced by the conjunction *that*.

Error Examples

WRONG: Steven wishes that he has a bigger apartment.
 RIGHT: Steven wishes that he *had* a bigger apartment.

WRONG: Helen wishes that she does not live in a dormitory.
 RIGHT: Helen wishes that she *did not* live in a dormitory.

WRONG: The actor wishes he was not required to perform every evening.
 RIGHT: The actor wishes he *were* not required to perform every evening.

WRONG: Ted wishes that he did not lose his job last month.
 RIGHT: Ted wishes that he *had not lost* his job last month.

WRONG: Bob wishes that he bought that house last spring.
 RIGHT: Bob wishes that he *had bought* that house last spring.

WRONG: I wish that I was living in a warmer climate.
 RIGHT: I wish that I *were* living in a warmer climate.

Exercise

Directions: Write a "C" on the line if the sentence is correct. Write an "X" on the line if there is an error in the verb that expresses a wish.

_____ **1.** They wish they were able to spend more time in London.

_____ **2.** My father wishes that he does not have to retire at age 65.

_____ **3.** The farmer wished that he does not lose money on his cotton crop.

_____ **4.** Abdulla wishes that his soccer team were the national champions.

_____ **5.** The doctor wishes that he has more free time to play golf.

_____ **6.** Each of her children wishes that he did not ignore the advice that she gave him.

_____ **7.** I wish that I was earning more money and working less time.

_____ **8.** My mother wishes that my father does more work around the house.

_____ **9.** We wish that we did not have to go to the library this Saturday.

_____ **10.** My friend Dorothy wishes she was still living in Paris.

Check your answers using the error key on page 75.

Conditionals

There are two kinds of conditions—*real* and *unreal*:

1. *Real* conditions are used for *possible* situations. The present tense is used in the *if*-clause (or conditional clause), and the future tense is used in the result clause.

    PRES.   FUT.
    If he *comes* to school, I *will give* him your message.
    (It is possible that he will come.)

2. *Unreal* conditions are used for *impossible* or *unreal* situations.

    ■ In present time, the past tense is used in the *if*-clause and *would*, *could*, or *might* + the simple verb (V) is used in the result clause.

        PAST   COULD + V
        If he *studied*, he *could get* good grades.
        (He doesn't study.)

        PAST   WOULD + V
        If he *came* to school, I *would give* him your message.
        (He doesn't come to school.)

    ■ In past time, the past perfect is used in the *if*-clause, and *would*, *could*, or *might* + *have* + the past participle are used in the result clause.

        PAST PERF.   WOULD + HAVE + PAST PART.
        If he *had come* to school, I *would have given* him your message.
        (He didn't come to school.)

Summary

If + present........... future (result)
If + past .... *would* + V (result)
If + past perfect...... *would* + *have* + past part. (result)

Notes   a. In general, avoid using *would* in the *if*-clause.

b. In present-time unreal *if*-clauses, the correct form of the verb *to be* for all persons is *were*.

If he *were* rich, he would go to Europe to study.

If I *were* you, I would study harder.

Error Examples

WRONG: If I will win the contest, I will buy a new car.
RIGHT: If I *win* the contest, I will buy a new car.

WRONG: If you had lost your job, what would you do?
RIGHT: If you *lost* your job, what would you do?

OR

If you had lost your job, what *would* you *have done*?

WRONG: If I had been there, I would make a speech.
RIGHT: If I *were* there, I would make a speech.

OR

If I had been there, I *would have made* a speech.

WRONG: If they had ask me, I would have given them my opinion.
RIGHT: If they had *asked* me, I would have given them my opinion.

WRONG: If Bob had studied more, he would have pass the test.
RIGHT: If Bob had studied more, he would have *passed* the test.

WRONG: If Jane had known it was supposed to rain, she would have took an umbrella.
RIGHT: If Jane had known it was supposed to rain, she would have *taken* an umbrella.

WRONG: If I would have a degree from that university, I would get a good job.
RIGHT: If I *had* a degree from that university, I would get a good job.

WRONG: If he would have been on time, we would have asked him to the party.
RIGHT: If he *had been* on time, we would have asked him to the party.

Exercise

Directions: Write a "C" on the line if the sentence is correct. Write an "X" on the line if there is an error in the use of the conditional.

_____ 1. If he had not tried to jump over the stream, he would not break his leg.

_____ 2. If he would be taller, he would be a good basketball player.

_____ 3. If my apartment would be larger, I would not have to move.

_____ 4. If he was ready, we would begin the lesson.

_____ 5. If classes had finished sooner, I would go to Canada last month.

_____ 6. If Betty would have driven more carefully, she would not have had that accident.

_____ 7. If I will finish studying, I will go to the movies with you.

_____ 8. If the king had known the truth, he would have been very angry.

_____ 9. If Bob had practiced playing tennis more, he will not have lost the game.

_____ 10. If he had been here earlier, I would have saw him.

_____ 11. If I had seen him, I would have reminded him about his appointment.

_____ 12. If you will take a trip this summer, where will you go?

_____ 13. If Bob had received his check on time, he had certainly bought a new suit.

_____ 14. If she were the only person available, we would have to hire her.

_____ 15. If she had told me that she did not have enough money, I would pay for her trip last summer.

Check your answers using the error key on page 75.

Modals

1. After all modals, use the simple form of the verb (V). The following is a list of modals:

can	could	must
may	should	will
might	would	shall

MODAL + V
They *can walk* five miles without getting tired.

MODAL + V
They *could walk* five miles without getting tired.

2. Use the past participle after the modal + *have*.

> MODAL + HAVE + PAST PART.
> Mr. and Mrs. Smith *might have enjoyed* the party.

> MODAL + HAVE + PAST PART.
> He *should have sent* in his application earlier.

> MODAL + HAVE + PAST PART.
> We *should* not *have eaten* such a big dinner.

3. When you change direct speech to indirect speech, *could*, *would*, *should*, and *might* do not change form.

DIRECT	**INDIRECT**
"You *should* always *do* your homework."	The teacher said that I *should always do* my homework.
"I *might ask* her out."	He said that he *might ask* her out.

4. Use *must have* + past participle for past conclusion only.

> The ground is wet; it *must have* rained. (conclusion)

5. Use *had* + infinitive for past obligation.

> I *had to go* to the dentist yesterday. (obligation)

Error Examples

WRONG: Beth must to take the bus yesterday because her car was being repaired.
RIGHT: Beth *had to take* the bus yesterday because her car was being repaired.

WRONG: We must to water our plants regularly.
RIGHT: We must *water* our plants regularly.

WRONG: They could walked to school because it was close.
RIGHT: They could *walk* to school because it was close.

WRONG: The show will have begin by the time we arrive.
RIGHT: The show will have *begun* by the time we arrive.

WRONG: John said that he might have gone to Harvard next year.
RIGHT: John said that he might *go* to Harvard next year.

Exercise

Directions: Write a "C" on the line if the sentence is correct. Write an "X" on the line if there is an error in the modals.

_____ **1.** My brother has to walk ten miles to buy some gas last weekend.

_____ **2.** There is no one outside the theater; the performance must have been cancelled.

_____ **3.** They must to sign up for that class by this Friday.

_____ **4.** We would have went to Florida, but it was having an unusual cold spell.

_____ **5.** Mrs. Jones told me that she might have baked a cake for my birthday tomorrow if she has time.

_____ **6.** Susan said she might leave before dinner.

_____ **7.** They might go to the store a few minutes ago.

_____ **8.** When my baby got very ill, I must have called the doctor immediately.

_____ **9.** The boys should not had made so much noise.

_____ **10.** I will be very happy when I graduate this year.

Check your answers with the error key on page 76.

Verbals

1. The following verbs can be followed by the infinitive (_to_ + V) as the direct object:

agree	forbid	mean
care	forget	offer
decide	hope	plan
deserve	intend	pretend
fail	learn	refuse

TO + V
Mr. Smith and Mr. Parker deserve _to be_ promoted.

TO + V
They decided _to leave_ early.

TO + V
The secretary offered _to come_ in early.

TO + V
He hopes _to see_ them again.

2. The following verbs can be followed by the gerund (V + *ing*) as the direct object:

admit	deny	postpone
appreciate	enjoy	practice
avoid	finish	stop
cannot help	keep	suggest
consider		

    V + ING
    She enjoyed *meeting* them.

    V + ING
    I have never considered *quitting* my job.

    V + ING
    He finishes *studying* every evening at ten.

    V + ING
    He admitted *committing* the crime.

3. The following verb phrases (verb + preposition) can be followed by the gerund (V + *ing*). Remember that gerunds, not infinitives, follow prepositions in general and not just the prepositions in this list. See also *Style—Prepositions in Combinations*, page 46.

be accustomed to	decide on	plan on
be interested in	get through	put off
be opposed to	keep on	think about
be used to	look forward to	think of

    PREP. + V + ING
    She was not used *to living* in a dormitory.

    PREP. + V + ING
    He kept *on driving* even though he was tired.

    PREP. + V + ING
    He has been looking forward *to meeting* you.

4. Use the simple form of the verb (V) after the causative verbs *let*, *make*, and *have* when the second verb is active.

    V
    He made the children *look* both ways before crossing the street.

    V
    The teacher let him *leave* early.

    V
    The teacher had the class *begin* to write a composition when the bell rang.

    Use a past participle after the causative verbs *have* and *get* when the second verb is passive in meaning.

    PAST PART.
    She had her passport *stamped* at the immigration office.

    PAST PART.
    They got their house *painted* last summer.

5. The following verbs of perception are followed by the simple form of the verb (V) *or* the present participle (V + *ing*):

feel   see
hear   smell
notice watch
observe

I heard the baby	OR	I heard the baby
V		V + ING
cry.		*crying.*
Jane observed him	OR	Jane observed him
V		V + ING
leave.		*leaving.*

Error Examples

WRONG: The professor forbids the students leaving early.
 RIGHT: The professor forbids the students *to leave* early.

WRONG: She could not help to laugh at his foolishness.
 RIGHT: She could not help *laughing* at his foolishness.

WRONG: I am opposed to go to war.
 RIGHT: I am opposed to *going* to war.

WRONG: Do not let those children to eat a lot of candy.
 RIGHT: Do not let those children *eat* a lot of candy.

WRONG: I was surprised to see a person to cry at that movie.
 RIGHT: I was surprised to see a person *cry* at that movie.

OR

I was surprised to see a person *crying* at that movie.

WRONG: She had her phone hook up when she returned from abroad.
 RIGHT: She had her phone *hooked up* when she returned from abroad.

WRONG: He had his annual chest X-ray taking yesterday.
 RIGHT: He had his annual chest X-ray *taken* yesterday.

Exercise

Directions: Write a "C" on the line if the sentence is correct. Write an "X" on the line if there is an error with the verbal (infinitive, gerund, simple verb, or participle) that follows the main verb.

_____ 1. Blocks from the stadium, we could hear the people to cheer.

_____ 2. Do you think you might enjoy living in a small town?

_____ 3. I always make the children to pick up their toys.

_____ 4. The official offered to help me get my papers in order.

_____ 5. I had the paperboy stop delivering papers for the month of July.

_____ 6. Since you need more money, you should not stop to try to find a better job.

_____ 7. He was not used to making decisions by himself.

_____ 8. Jane had her blood pressure taking recently.

_____ 9. What made the student decide leaving early?

_____ 10. I am looking forward to see you again soon.

_____ 11. What do you think of our having a party to celebrate?

_____ 12. She had her shoes dyed to match her dress.

_____ 13. She could not help noticing the man to cry.

_____ 14. One should avoid eating a heavy meal late in the evening.

_____ 15. We had Tom to make the dinner reservations.

_____ 16. Since he promised to take care of it, his parents let the boy to buy a dog.

_____ 17. He was not used to living alone.

_____ 18. Bob had his gas and electricity turn on when he moved into his new apartment last week.

_____ 19. When will you get through to read that book?

_____ 20. The doctor had Mrs. Jones take ten pills a day for her heart.

_____ 21. Their boss never has them to stay past 5:00 p.m.

_____ 22. They saw the thief running from the bank.

_____ 23. The professor had us to read the first half of the book by Monday.

_____ 24. Please do not fail registering before the deadline.

_____ 25. As I entered the house, I smelled the food cooking.

_____ 26. We had our university identification pictures taken yesterday.

_____ 27. The law of that country forbids anyone under eighteen driving a car.

_____ **28.** The teacher made us using our imaginations.

_____ **29.** The class could not help to laugh when the teacher dropped all his papers.

_____ **30.** When we decided to stay in Mexico longer, we had our visas renewed.

Check your answers using the error key on page 76.

Past Participles

The past participle is used in the following:

1. *Present Perfect*

   PAST PART.
   He has *broken* the world's track record.

2. *Past Perfect*

   PAST PART.
   Mary had *spoken* to John about the matter before I arrived.

3. *Unreal Past Conditional*

   PAST PART.   PAST PART.
   If he had *been* here on time, he would have *heard* the news.

4. *Passive*

   PAST PART.
   The president's reelection was *taken* for granted by his constituents.

5. *Perfect Infinitive*

   PAST PART.
   I would like to have *grown* up on a farm.

6. *Perfect Participle*

   PAST PART.
   Having *swum* ten laps in the Olympic pool, he was exhausted.

7. *Adjective*

   PAST PART.
   The *stolen* watch was a very expensive piece of jewelry.

8. *Past Modal*

   PAST PART.
   Molly said that I should not have *gone* to that movie.

9. *Introductory Verbal Phrase*

   PAST PART.
   Seen from a distance, the house appeared to be in good condition.

Notes   The following are some of the verbs in English whose past participle forms (with the exception of *hurt* and *hear*) are *different from the past tense forms*.

Verb	Past Participle
be	been
begin	begun
break	broken
choose	chosen
do	done
drink	drunk
drive	driven
eat	eaten
fly	flown
forgive	forgiven
give	given
go	gone
grow	grown
hear	heard
hurt	hurt
know	known
ride	ridden
ring	rung
run	run
see	seen
show	shown
sing	sung
speak	spoken
steal	stolen
swim	swum
take	taken
tear	torn
throw	thrown
wear	worn
write	written

Error Examples

WRONG: He has sang in the choir for ten years.
 RIGHT: He has *sung* in the choir for ten years.

WRONG: I saw him after he had ran for five miles.
 RIGHT: I saw him after he had *run* for five miles.

WRONG: The president's large black limousine was drived by a chauffeur.
 RIGHT: The president's large black limousine was *driven* by a chauffeur.

WRONG: Children are to be saw and not heard.
 RIGHT: Children are to be *seen* and not heard.

WRONG: Having heared the joke before, I did not find it funny the second time.
 RIGHT: Having *heard* the joke before, I did not find it funny the second time.

WRONG: The class could have began on time if the teacher had not been late.
 RIGHT: The class could have *begun* on time if the teacher had not been late.

WRONG: The breaked lamp was lying in little pieces on the rug.
 RIGHT: The *broken* lamp was lying in little pieces on the rug.

Exercise

Directions: Write a "C" on the line if the sentence is correct. Write an "X" on the line if there is an error with the past participle.

_____ 1. By the time Joan arrived, all of the food had been ate.

_____ 2. Having stolen the money, the thief ran down the street as fast as he could.

_____ 3. John had gave his speech when Bob was finally able to get to the meeting.

_____ 4. Wrote in 1847, the opera has never enjoyed popular success.

_____ 5. The professor told the class that they should have known the correct answer.

_____ 6. Claire has not wore her new coat since she came to Florida.

_____ 7. Betty began to cry when she realized that her new dress was torn.

_____ 8. Never having flied before, Mark was very excited as he drove to the airport.

_____ 9. I would like to have rang the bell earlier.

_____ 10. If he had shown the official his passport, he would not have had any problems.

_____ 11. She has began to look like her mother.

_____ 12. That old horse has been ridden by children for years.

_____ 13. I would not have did it if he had not made me nervous.

_____ 14. The broke chair had only three legs.

_____ 15. He claims to have hurted his leg in the game last night.

Check your answers using the error key on page 76.

Present and Perfect Participles and Infinitives

1. Present participles (V + *ing*) in introductory verb phrases express action of the *same time* as the main verb.

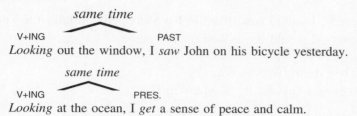

    Looking out the window, I *saw* John on his bicycle yesterday.

    Looking at the ocean, I *get* a sense of peace and calm.

2. Perfect participles (*having* + past participle) in introductory verb phrases express action that occurred prior to the main verb's action.

        PERF. PART.   PAST
    Having taken a shower, I *went* to bed. (I took a shower *before* I went to bed.)

        PERF. PART.   PRES.
    Having lost all our money, we *have* to return from our vacation early.
    (We lost our money, and now we have to go home early.)

3. The present infinitive (*to* + V) expresses action that occurs at the same time as or future to the main verb.

            PRES.
        PRES. INFIN.
    I *hope to pass* the test tomorrow. (*To pass* is future to *hope*.)

            PRES.
        PRES. INFIN.
    I *wanted to leave* early yesterday. (*To leave* is same time as or future to *wanted*.)

4. The perfect infinitive (*to* + *have* + past participle) expresses action that occurred prior to the main verb's action.

        PRES.   PERF. INFIN.
    I *hope to have passed* the test I took yesterday.
    (I hope now that I passed the test I took yesterday.)

            PRES.   PERF. INFIN.
    He *is reported to have died* yesterday.
    (He apparently died yesterday and now his death is being reported.)

            PAST   PERF. INFIN.
    He *was reported to have died* the day before.
    (He apparently died the day before his death was reported.)

        PRES.   PERF. INFIN.
    I *would like to have lived* in the seventeenth century.
    (I wish now that I had lived at some time in the past.)

Error Examples

WRONG: Getting a driver's license, Paul was able to drive from Boston to Los Angeles.
 RIGHT: *Having gotten* a driver's license, Paul was able to drive from Boston to Los Angeles.

WRONG: When I saw you yesterday, I would have liked to have stopped and talked to you.
 RIGHT: When I saw you yesterday, I would have liked to *stop* and *talk* to you.

WRONG: She is reputed to be a spy during World War II.
 RIGHT: She is reputed *to have been* a spy during World War II.

WRONG: He is said to having written a great novel.
 RIGHT: He is said *to have written* a great novel.

Exercise

Directions: Write a "C" on the line if the sentence is correct. Write an "X" on the line if there is an error in the participle or the infinitive.

_____ **1.** They chose not to have attended the meeting.

_____ **2.** She would have liked to study abroad.

_____ **3.** The notorious criminal is reported to having surrendered yesterday.

_____ **4.** Applying at the University of Arizona, she anxiously awaited her acceptance.

_____ **5.** They are presumed to die in the crash last weekend.

_____ **6.** Having studied diligently, he found the examination quite easy.

_____ **7.** Writing the letter, she mailed it on her way to work.

_____ **8.** The police officer wanted to give me a ride home.

_____ **9.** Catching several fish, they cooked them for dinner.

_____ **10.** Betty should have remembered to call me last night.

Check your answers using the error key on page 76.

Chapter Quiz

Part A

Directions: Write a "C" on the line if the sentence is correct. Write an "X" on the line if there is an error in the verb.

_____ **1.** Mr. and Mrs. Jones stopped smoking a year ago and have not started again.

_____ **2.** After jogging, I was so hungry that I could have ate a horse.

_____ **3.** Many people who were opposed to use nuclear energy in any form demonstrated against the opening of the new nuclear power plant.

_____ **4.** The license bureau demands that a person renew his license before it expires.

_____ **5.** For several years now, the student body is attempting to gain more influence over university policies.

_____ **6.** If I will get the money in time, I will go to California on my next vacation.

_____ **7.** After agreeing to make the necessary changes in the contract, Mr. Martin had his secretary type the amended version for us to sign.

_____ **8.** Much to his surprise, when Robert arrived in London, he had found several relatives waiting for him at the airport.

_____ **9.** Reading several books on that subject, Bill considered himself an expert.

_____ **10.** Ralph wishes that he went to the bank this morning before he went to work.

Check your answers using the error key on page 77.

Part B

Directions: In the Sentence Completion questions, one or more words are left out of each sentence. Under each sentence, you will see four words or phrases. Select the one word or phrase that completes the sentence correctly, then write it in the space provided in the book or on a separate sheet of paper.

1. They told me that I _____ the tap water in that country.

(A) must not have drank
(B) could not drunk
(C) should not have drunk
(D) could have drink

2. The doctor was very surprised that his patient had let his condition _____ so much before calling him.

(A) deteriorate
(B) to deteriorate
(C) to deteriorating
(D) deteriorating

3. If he had applied by August 15, the university _____ him this semester.

   (A) would accepted
   (B) had accepted
   (C) should have accept
   (D) would have accepted

4. When we finally bought stock in that company, the market _____ its peak and the stock was declining in value.

   (A) did already reach
   (B) has already reached
   (C) was already reached
   (D) had already reached

5. They are said _____ a dynamic new play.

   (A) to have wrote
   (B) to have written
   (C) to have writing
   (D) have written

6. Last year in the middle of the most severe drought in recent history, the already dwindling tribe _____ finally to leave its ancestral land and to look for a new place to live.

   (A) had decided
   (B) decided
   (C) has decided
   (D) decides

7. It was important that they _____ before the curtain went up last night.

   (A) arrive
   (B) have arrived
   (C) arrived
   (D) had arrived

8. I could see Susan's hands _____ slightly as she placed her papers on the podium and prepared to address the audience.

   (A) to tremble
   (B) trembles
   (C) trembled
   (D) trembling

9. The babysitter agreed _____ the children before putting them to bed.

   (A) for bathing
   (B) to bath
   (C) to bathe
   (D) to giving a bath

10. When the famous pianist was a child, he was accustomed to _____ for several hours a day.

    (A) practice
    (B) practicing
    (C) practiced
    (D) be practicing

Check your answers using the error key on page 77.

ERROR KEYS

(All references to rules and notes refer to the specific section where the quiz appears.)

Tense

__X__ **1.** (I *was* in Mexico). See rule 2.

__C__ **2.**

__X__ **3.** (He *was* a student). See rule 2.

__C__ **4.**

__X__ **5.** (and *went* to lunch). See rule 2.

__C__ **6.**

__X__ **7.** (they *recognized* us). See rule 2.

__C__ **8.**

__X__ **9.** (*has seen* ten patients). See rule 1.

__X__ **10.** (He *has studied* English). See rule 1.

Time Clauses

__X__ **1.** (when it *is* spring)

__X__ **2.** (when winter *comes*)

__C__ **3.**

__X__ **4.** (the children *visit* their grandmother)

__C__ **5.**

__X__ **6.** (when you *are* in Scotland)

__X__ **7.** (critics *see*)

__C__ **8.**

__C__ **9.**

__X__ **10.** (Joan *gets*)

Verbs of "Demand"

__X__ **1.** (employees *take*)

__C__ **2.**

__X__ **3.** (that I *stop* smoking)

__C__ **4.**

__X__ **5.** (that John *have*)

__X__ **6.** (that his crew *have*)

__C__ **7.**

__X__ **8.** (that Mr. Smith *not leave*) See Notes.

__C__ **9.**

__X__ **10.** (that a driver *renew*)

Wishes

__C__ **1.**

__X__ **2.** (he *did not* have to). See rule 1.

__X__ **3.** (he *had not* lost). See rule 3.

__C__ **4.**

__X__ **5.** (that he *had*). See rule 1.

__X__ **6.** (he *had not ignored*). See rule 3.

__X__ **7.** (that I *were* earning). See rule 2.

__X__ **8.** (father *did*). See rule 1.

__C__ **9.**

__X__ **10.** (she *were* still living). See rule 2.

Conditionals

__X__ **1.** (he would not *have broken*) See rule 2. See also *Verbs—Past Participles*, page 68.

__X__ **2.** (If he *were* taller). See rule 2 and note b.

__X__ **3.** (If my apartment *were* larger). See rule 2 and note b.

__X__ **4.** (If he *were* ready). See rule 2 and note b.

__X__ **5.** (I *would have gone*). See rule 2.

__X__ **6.** (If Betty *had driven*). See rule 2 and note a.

__X__ **7.** (If *I finish*). See rule 1.

__C__ **8.**

__X__ **9.** (he *would* not have lost). See rule 2.

__X__ **10.** (I would have *seen* him). See rule 2. See also *Verbs—Past Participles*, page 68.

__C__ **11.**

__X__ **12.** (If *you take*). See rule 1.

__X__ **13.** (he *would* certainly *have bought*). See rule 2.

__C__ **14.**

__X__ **15.** (I *would have paid*). See rule 2.

Modals

_____X_____ **1.** (*had* to walk). See rule 5.

_____C_____ **2.**

_____X_____ **3.** (must *sign up*). See rule 1.

_____X_____ **4.** (would have *gone*). See rule 2. See also *Verbs—Past Participles*, page 68.

_____X_____ **5.** (might *bake*). See rule 3.

_____C_____ **6.**

_____X_____ **7.** (might *have gone*). See rule 2.

_____X_____ **8.** (I *had to call*). See rule 4.

_____X_____ **9.** (should not *have* made). See rule 1.

_____C_____ **10.**

Verbals

_____X_____ **1.** (hear the people *cheer*) OR (hear the people *cheering*). See rule 5.

_____C_____ **2.**

_____X_____ **3.** (make the children *pick up*). See rule 4.

_____C_____ **4.**

_____C_____ **5.**

_____X_____ **6.** (stop *trying* to find). See rule 2.

_____C_____ **7.**

_____X_____ **8.** (pressure *taken* recently). See rule 4.

_____X_____ **9.** (decide to *leave* early). See rule 1.

_____X_____ **10.** (looking forward to *seeing*). See rule 3.

_____C_____ **11.**

_____C_____ **12.**

_____X_____ **13.** (noticing the man *cry*) OR (noticing the man *crying*). See rule 5.

_____C_____ **14.**

_____X_____ **15.** (Tom *make* the dinner). See rule 4.

_____X_____ **16.** (let the boy *buy*). See rule 4.

_____C_____ **17.**

_____X_____ **18.** (electricity *turned on* when). See rule 4.

_____X_____ **19.** (get through *reading*). See rule 3.

_____C_____ **20.**

_____X_____ **21.** (has them *stay*). See rule 4.

_____C_____ **22.**

_____X_____ **23.** (had us *read* the first). See rule 4.

_____X_____ **24.** (do not fail *to register*). See rule 1.

_____C_____ **25.**

_____C_____ **26.**

_____X_____ **27.** (forbids anyone under eighteen *to drive*). See rule 1.

_____X_____ **28.** (made us *use* our). See rule 4.

_____X_____ **29.** (could not help *laughing*). See rule 2.

_____C_____ **30.**

Past Participles

_____X_____ **1.** (had been *eaten*). See rule 4 and note.

_____C_____ **2.**

_____X_____ **3.** (had *given* his speech). See rule 2 and note.

_____X_____ **4.** (*Written* in 1847). See rule 9 and note.

_____C_____ **5.**

_____X_____ **6.** (has not *worn*). See rule 1 and note.

_____C_____ **7.**

_____X_____ **8.** (Never having *flown*). See rule 6 and note.

_____X_____ **9.** (to have *rung*). See rule 5 and note.

_____C_____ **10.**

_____X_____ **11.** (She has *begun*). See rule 1 and note.

_____C_____ **12.**

_____X_____ **13.** (would not have *done*). See rule 3 and note.

_____X_____ **14.** (*broken* chair). See rule 7 and note.

_____X_____ **15.** (to have *hurt*). See rule 5 and note.

Present and Perfect Participles and Infinitives

_____X_____ **1.** (chose not *to attend*). See rule 3.

_____C_____ **2.**

_____X_____ **3.** (to *have* surrendered). See rule 4.

_____X_____ **4.** (*Having applied*). See rule 2.

_____X_____ **5.** (to *have died*). See rule 4.

_____C_____ **6.**

_____X_____ **7.** (*Having written*). See rule 2.

_____C_____ **8.**

_____X_____ **9.** (*Having caught*). See rule 2.

_____C_____ **10.**

Chapter Quiz

Part A

C 1.

X 2. (could have *eaten*). See *Past Participles*, page 68.

X 3. (opposed to *using*). See *Verbals*, page 64.

C 4.

X 5. (*has been* attempting). See *Tense*, page 55.

X 6. (If I *get*). See *Conditionals*, page 60.

C 7.

X 8. (he *found*). See *Tense*, page 55.

X 9. (*Having read*). See *Present and Perfect Participles* and *Infinitives*, page 71.

X 10. (that he *had gone*). See *Wishes*, page 59.

Part B

(C) 1. (A) See *Modals*, page 62.
(B) See *Modals*, page 62.
(C) Correct
(D) See *Modals*, page 62.

(A) 2. **(A) Correct**
(B) See *Verbals*, page 64.
(C) See *Verbals*, page 64.
(D) See *Verbals*, page 64.

(D) 3. (A) See *Conditionals*, page 60.
(B) See *Conditionals*, page 60.
(C) See *Conditionals*, page 60.
(D) Correct

(D) 4. (A) See *Tense*, page 55.
(B) See *Tense*, page 55.
(C) See *Tense*, page 55.
(D) Correct

(B) 5. (A) See *Present and Perfect Participles* and *Infinitives*, page 71.
(B) Correct
(C) See *Present and Perfect Participles* and *Infinitives*, page 71.
(D) See *Present and Perfect Participles* and *Infinitives*, page 71.

(B) 6. (A) See *Tense*, page 55.
(B) Correct
(C) See *Tense*, page 55.
(D) See *Tense*, page 55.

(A) 7. **(A) Correct**
(B) See *Verbs of "Demand,"* page 57.
(C) See *Verbs of "Demand,"* page 57.
(D) See *Verbs of "Demand,"* page 57.

(D) 8. (A) See *Verbals*, page 64.
(B) See *Verbals*, page 64.
(C) See *Verbals*, page 64.
(D) Correct

(C) 9. (A) See *Verbals*, page 64.
(B) See *Verbals*, page 64.
(C) Correct
(D) See *Verbals*, page 64.

(B) 10. (A) See *Verbals*, page 64.
(B) Correct
(C) See *Verbals*, page 64.
(D) See *Verbals*, page 64.

Pronouns

5

Relative Pronouns

Who, *whom*, *which*, *that*, and *whose* are relative pronouns used to introduce relative clauses (adjective clauses). For the *who/whom* problem, see page 83.

1. *Who* and *whom* are used for people.

    I saw the man *who* is famous for inventing plastic.

    Give it to the man *whom* you already know.

2. *Which* is used for nonrestrictive, or nonessential, clauses; that is, clauses that are not essential to the meaning of the sentence. Note that nonessential clauses are always preceded and followed by a comma.

    The 104 bus, *which* is always late, should arrive at 4 p.m. at the shopping center.

3. *That* is used for restrictive, or essential clauses. You do not use a comma with essential clauses.

    Here is the man *that* can answer your questions.

    Did you find the book *that* you wanted to buy?

4. *Whose* is used to show possession. It can be followed by persons or things.

    This is the man *whose* car was towed away.

    Do you know the doctor *whose* children I teach?

Error Examples

WRONG: He is the student which always arrives late.
 RIGHT: He is the student *who* always arrives late.

           OR

    He is the student *that* always arrives late.

WRONG: Saudi Arabia is a country who exports oil all over the world.
 RIGHT: Saudi Arabia is a country *that* exports oil all over the world.

WRONG: We visited the building what is famous for its unusual design.
 RIGHT: We visited the building, which is famous for its unusual design.

           OR

    We visited the building *that* is famous for its unusual design.

WRONG: There was a story in the paper about the man that his car was stolen.
 RIGHT: There was a story in the paper about the man *whose* car was stolen.

Exercise

Directions: Write a "C" on the line if the sentence is correct. Write an "X" on the line if there is an error in the relative pronoun.

_____ **1.** I like novels who deal with philosophical questions.

_____ **2.** The company did not want to hire a man that his experience was so limited.

_____ **3.** The family whose house burned down was on television.

_____ **4.** She wore a dress what everyone considered extravagant.

_____ **5.** The train, which goes to Flower Square, will arrive at any moment.

_____ **6.** The ship that we boarded in Rio was bound for Marseilles.

_____ **7.** John did not want to do business with a man which had been in prison.

_____ **8.** Take your car back to the man who sold it to you.

_____ **9.** That is the baby which has been in the incubator for three months.

_____ **10.** The woman that her photograph was in the paper is making a speech at the town hall tonight.

Check your answers using the error key on page 95.

Personal Pronouns—Case

1. Subject pronouns (*I*, *you*, *he*, *she*, *it*, *we*, and *they*) are used in the subject position and after the verb *to be*.

   S
   They arrived safely last night.

   BE + S PRON.
   It *was they* who knocked on the door last night.

2. Object pronouns (*me*, *you*, *him*, *her*, *it*, *us*, and *them*) are used as objects of verbs and prepositions and as subjects of infinitives.

   VERB OBJ.
   I *told him* the news.

   PREP.   OBJ.
   Between you and me, the economic situation looks bad.

   S   INFIN.
   We asked *him to bring* a salad to the party.

Notes a. Pronouns in apposition* are in the same case as the pronouns they follow. Example: Let's (Let us), *you and me*, go dancing Friday night. *Us* is the object of *let*. *You* and *me* must also be in the objective case.

b. Pronouns after the conjunctions *as* or *than* should be subject pronouns when they function as subjects.

$$\overset{s}{}$$
He is as tall as *I* (am tall).

$$\overset{s}{}$$
John plays soccer as well as *he* (plays soccer).

$$\overset{s}{}$$
They are more diligent students than *we* (are).

c. The correct forms of the reflexive pronouns for *him* and *them* are *himself* and *themselves*, NOT *hisself* or *theirselves*.

Error Examples

WRONG: Jane and him planned to go to the movies.
RIGHT: Jane and *he* planned to go to the movies.

WRONG: She sold the car to Mary and he.
RIGHT: She sold the car to Mary and *him*.

WRONG: I never met a man as kind as him.
RIGHT: I never met a man as kind as *he*.

WRONG: For you and I arriving on time will be difficult.
RIGHT: For you and *me* arriving on time will be difficult.

WRONG: He specifically told them, Bob and he, to get ready.
RIGHT: He specifically told them, Bob and *him*, to get ready.

WRONG: Several times during the semester the teacher asked he to speak to the class.
RIGHT: Several times during the semester the teacher asked *him* to speak to the class.

WRONG: Ask him to do it hisself.
RIGHT: Ask him to do it *himself*.

WRONG: They do not want to go by theirselves.
RIGHT: They do not want to go by *themselves*.

---

* An *appositive* is a noun or pronoun that follows another noun or pronoun and identifies the first noun or pronoun.

Exercise

Directions: Write a "C" on the line if the sentence is correct. Write an "X" on the line if there is an error in pronoun case.

_____ **1.** I was surprised to learn that Betty and him were hurt in the accident.

_____ **2.** I often remember when Paul and I visited Rome.

_____ **3.** He moved the furniture by hisself.

_____ **4.** She gave us, Margaret and I, the notes we missed in class.

_____ **5.** They were sitting by themselves next to the swimming pool.

_____ **6.** That project is the responsibility of Susan and she.

_____ **7.** Let us keep this secret between you and me.

_____ **8.** Do not forget to give the message to Bob and me.

_____ **9.** The tourists asked us, my cousin and me, how to get to the museum.

_____ **10.** Please be sure to notify my husband or I when the package arrives.

_____ **11.** The children assembled the toy house by theirselves.

_____ **12.** How often do you have the opportunity to meet a man as intelligent as him?

_____ **13.** For the majority of us the issue is rather confusing.

_____ **14.** Mary will never be as rich as I.

_____ **15.** It is her, the one whom nobody likes.

Check your answers using the error key on page 95.

Who/Whom

Who and *whoever* are subject pronouns
   Whom and *whomever* are object pronouns.

1. In general, the patterns for *who* and *whoever* are:

   ■ **who (whoever) + verb**

   S
   WHO + VERB
   The woman *who sang* yesterday has studied voice for years.

   S
   WHO + VERB
   Who came to the party?

   S
   WHOEVER + VERB
   Give the money to *whoever needs* it.

   S
   WHOEVER + VERB
   I said that *whoever had finished* could leave.

   ■ **whom (whomever) + subject + verb**

   OBJ.
   WHOM + S + VERB
   The woman *whom I met* yesterday is a voice teacher.

   OBJ.
   WHOMEVER + S + VERB
   Give it to *whomever you like*.

2. Sometimes expressions like the following separate *who* (*whoever*) or *whom* (*whomever*) from its own verb or subject and verb:

   "I think"
   "she said"
   "we know"
   "do you know"

   S
   WHO   VERB
   He is a student *who we believe can do* the job.

   S
   WHO   VERB
   Give the job to the person *who you think is* best suited for it.

   OBJ.
   WHOM   S + VERB
   He is a man *whom I feel you can trust*.

   S
   WHOEVER   VERB
   Tell the story to *whoever you think should hear it*.

Error Examples

WRONG: I saw the man who John spoke to.
  RIGHT: I saw the man *whom* John spoke to.

WRONG: Do not speak to people whom are strangers.
  RIGHT: Do not speak to people *who* are strangers.

WRONG: Take your problem to the person whom you think can help you.
  RIGHT: Take your problem to the person *who* you think can help you.

WRONG: She gave it to the only person who she believed.
  RIGHT: She gave it to the only person *whom* she believed.

WRONG: They will award the prize to whomever is best.
  RIGHT: They will award the prize to *whoever* is best.

WRONG: They chose whomever was most interested.
  RIGHT: They chose *whoever* was most interested.

Exercise

> **Directions:** Write a "C" on the line if the sentence is correct. Write an "X" on the line if there is a *who/whom* error.

_____ **1.** I met the new people whom I thought were from your country.

_____ **2.** You should ask advice from people who you trust.

_____ **3.** Ask whoever is willing to come early.

_____ **4.** There is the new director who I think you met before.

_____ **5.** The man who you think is a doctor is actually a male nurse.

_____ **6.** She was the person who the teacher chose to speak at the final ceremony.

_____ **7.** It is pleasant to be with people who like us and whom we like.

_____ **8.** Ask anyone who you think is interested to join the team.

_____ **9.** Whom do you think will be ready on time?

_____ **10.** Take this to whomever the supervisor chose to do the job.

_____ **11.** The lawyer whom handled that case disappeared.

_____ **12.** Assign this project to whoever you like.

_____ **13.** Deliver this envelope to whomever answers the door.

_____ **14.** It was Jack and I who he thought were at fault in the situation.

_____ **15.** Many women whom are working would prefer to be at home.

Check your answers using the error key on page 95.

Possessives

Use the possessive case* with gerunds (V + *ing* used as a noun).

> POSSESSIVE V + ING
> I resented *their interrupting* our conversations.

> POSSESSIVE V + ING
> *His swimming* is getting a lot better.

> POSS. V + ING
> Because of *your leaving* late, you will have to take a taxi in order to catch your train.

Notes   *It's* is *not* a possessive pronoun but a contraction of *it is*.

Error Examples

WRONG: Susan did not like him making a lot of noise while she was studying.
RIGHT: Susan did not like *his* making a lot of noise while she was studying.

WRONG: Betty cannot remember you telling her that story.
RIGHT: Betty cannot remember *your* telling her that story.

WRONG: They did not like him calling so late at night.
RIGHT: They did not like *his* calling so late at night.

WRONG: I approve of one living on his own before marriage.
RIGHT: I approve of *one's* living on his own before marriage.

WRONG: I could not sleep last night because of them shouting next door.
RIGHT: I could not sleep last night because of *their* shouting next door.

WRONG: The chairman congratulated us on us winning the contest.
RIGHT: The chairman congratulated us on *our* winning the contest.

WRONG: When we had a dog, I can remember it chasing birds.
RIGHT: When we had a dog, I can remember *its* chasing birds.

WRONG: Professor Jones was angry at me coming late to class every day.
RIGHT: Professor Jones was angry at *my* coming late to class every day.

---

* Remember that the possessive pronouns are *my*, *your*, *his*, *her*, *its*, *our*, *their*, and *one's*.

Exercise

Directions: Write a "C" on the line if the sentence is correct. Write an "X" on the line if there is an error with the possessive pronoun.

_____ 1. Our neighbors complained about our playing the stereo too loudly.

_____ 2. I sadly thought of you saying good-bye.

_____ 3. Were you surprised at their buying a new car?

_____ 4. I cannot imagine his refusing that job.

_____ 5. What did you think of them leaving so abruptly?

_____ 6. My neighbor has a lovely cat, but it meowing bothers me at night.

_____ 7. Him playing the drums day and night made his roommates very angry.

_____ 8. Her winning first prize delighted us a great deal.

_____ 9. I really appreciate your trying to arrive on time.

_____ 10. Mrs. Allen was concerned about me having to drive so far every day.

_____ 11. Your telling him that might disturb him a great deal.

_____ 12. His family was elated when they heard of him winning the race.

_____ 13. Mr. Smith was upset by their fast driving.

_____ 14. Did the teacher mind us whispering in the back of the room?

_____ 15. My boss finally approved of me taking my vacation in August.

Check your answers using the error key on page 95.

Faulty Reference

The antecedent* of a pronoun must be *clearly* understood.

ANTECEDENT   PRON.
When *Betty* was in college, *she* wrote to her family every week. (*She* clearly refers to *Betty*.)

ANTECEDENT   PRON.
As *Bob* got off the plane, *he* waved to his father.
(*He* clearly refers to *Bob*.)

                    ANTECEDENT   PRON.
As Don explained his *theory* to me, I found *it* fascinating.
(*It* clearly refers to *theory*.)

---

* An *antecedent* is the noun or pronoun to which a pronoun refers.

Error Examples

WRONG: Mary told Paula that she had to read Plato's *Republic*.
        (*She* can refer to *Mary* or *Paula*.)
 RIGHT: Mary told Paula, "I have to read Plato's *Republic*."

WRONG: Paul saw his friend as he was walking across the campus.
        (*He* can refer to *Paul* or *his friend*.)
 RIGHT: While Paul was walking across the campus, he saw his friend.

WRONG: Sylvia and Mary saw a movie yesterday, and she said it was wonderful.
        (*She* can refer to *Sylvia* or *Mary*.)
 RIGHT: Sylvia and Mary saw a movie yesterday, and Sylvia said it was wonderful.

WRONG: I put the vase on the glass table and it broke.
        (*It* can refer to *vase* or *table*.)
 RIGHT: The vase broke as I put it on the glass table.

WRONG: In the book it says to cook the meat for several hours.
        (*It* has *no* antecedent in this context.)
 RIGHT: *The book* says to cook the meat for several hours.

Exercise

Directions: Write a "C" on the line if the sentence is correct. Write an "X" on the line if the pronoun does not clearly refer to one antecedent or if it has no antecedent.

_____ **1.** Mr. Smith told Mr. Jones that he had lost a lot of money in the stock market.

_____ **2.** In the telephone directory, it says to call directory assistance in that situation.

_____ **3.** When Peter finished the examination, he gave it to the professor.

_____ **4.** Cathy saw her friend as she was driving home from work.

_____ **5.** When John put a new frame on the picture, it looked strange.

_____ **6.** The laundry was not dry enough for Susan to bring it into the house.

_____ **7.** He put all his savings in the stock market, and it suffered great losses that year.

_____ **8.** When Jack was in the navy, he learned electronics.

_____ **9.** In the newspaper it says there is renewed interest in the silver market.

_____ **10.** The A Team played the B Team yesterday, and now it is in first place.

Check your answers using the error key on page 96.

Person

Do not carelessly change the person of a pronoun.

> PRON.
> A *student* has to expect to work hard when *he* goes to college.

OR

> A student has to expect to work hard when *she* goes to college.

> PRON.
> *One* should brush *one's* teeth twice daily.

OR

> PRON.
> One should brush *his* teeth twice daily.

| Notes | a. A *student*, a *person*, or *one* can use the following third-person singular pronouns: *he*, *she*, or *he or she*; *him*, *her*, or *him or her*; and *his*, *her*, or *his or her*. |

> A student must renew *his or her* library card every year.

b. The possessive pronoun for *one* can be *one's* or *his or her* (see also note a) but never *ones*.

Error Examples

WRONG: A person can expect to receive a traffic ticket when we drive too fast.
RIGHT: A person can expect to receive a traffic ticket when *he* drives too fast.

WRONG: When one has a toothache, you should go to the dentist.
RIGHT: When one has a toothache, *one* should go to the dentist.

WRONG: One should remember to pay your telephone bill on time.
RIGHT: One should remember to pay *one's* telephone bill on time.

WRONG: One should have ones teeth checked regularly.
RIGHT: One should have *one's* teeth checked regularly.

Exercise

Directions: Write a "C" on the line if the sentence is correct. Write an "X" on the line if there is an error with the person of the pronoun.

_____ 1. When a person eats well, you feel well.

_____ 2. For successful completion of this exercise, one must give his complete attention to the task at hand.

_____ 3. One should always pay your rent promptly.

_____ 4. One should never forget his obligations to his family.

_____ 5. One often forgets one's early failures.

_____ 6. When a person is learning to play a musical instrument, we must practice several hours a day.

_____ 7. When one goes through life, we meet many challenges.

_____ 8. One can always rely on one's friends in time of need.

_____ 9. When a person goes to a foreign country, he must expect many things to be different.

_____ 10. When you find yourself in an air-conditioned theater, one often wishes he had a sweater.

Check your answers with the error key on page 96.

Number*

1. Pronouns must agree in number with their *antecedents* (the noun or pronoun to which they refer).

   ANTECEDENT   PRON.
   Many of the people in Ubudu live *their* whole lives in poverty.

   ANTECEDENT   PRON.
   A *person* should love *his* parents.

   ANTECEDENT   PRON.
   Great *music* can inspire and move people with *its* beauty.

---

* Note to student: It is advisable to study this section *after* you study *Subject-Verb Agreement*, page 141.

2. The following indefinite pronouns are singular and take singular pronouns: *each*, *either*, *neither*, *one* and all words ending in *-one*, *-body*, or *-thing*, such as *anybody*, *nothing*, and *everybody*.

>   ANTECEDENT   PRON.
> *Each* of the women took off *her* hat.

>   ANTECEDENT   PRON.
> *Everyone* should bring *their* book to class.

>   ANTECEDENT   PRON.
> I knew *one* of the students, but I could not remember *her* name.

>   ANTECEDENT   PRON.
> *Nobody* in that office knows what *he* is supposed to do.

>   ANTECEDENT   PRON.   PRON.
> *Everyone* in the class should do *her* own work *herself*.

3. When compound subjects are joined by *neither . . . nor* or *either . . . or*, the pronoun will agree with the subject nearer the verb.

>   S   S (nearer the verb)   PRON.
> Neither my *mother* nor my *sisters* could lend me *their* sewing machine.

>   S   S (nearer the verb)   PRON.
> Either my *sisters* or my *mother* will lend me *her* typewriter.

4. Some words appear to be plural but are actually singular. Some of these are: *physics*, *mathematics*, *economics*, *news*, and *politics*.

>   ANTECEDENT   PRON.
> *Politics* interests me as *it* affects the economy.

Error Examples

WRONG: Modern music, including disco and rock n'roll, reflects modern society in their themes and musical qualities.

 RIGHT: Modern music, including disco and rock n'roll, reflects modern society in *its* themes and musical qualities.

>   (The antecedent of *its* is *music*.)

WRONG: Every woman can find their place in the world.

 RIGHT: Every woman can find *her* place in the world.

>   (The antecedent of *her* is *woman*.)

WRONG: Neither the stars nor the moon shone their light on us.

 RIGHT: Neither the stars nor the moon shone *its* light on us.

>   (The antecedent of *its* is *moon*.)

WRONG: Either Paul or his parents will let me use his car.

 RIGHT: Either Paul or his parents will let me use *their* car.

>   (The antecedent of *their* is *parents*.)

WRONG: Every one of the students wrote their names on the paper.
RIGHT: Every one of the students wrote *his name* on the paper.
(The antecedent of *his* is *one*.)

WRONG: Each of the boys should have their teeth checked.
RIGHT: Each of the boys should have *his* teeth checked.
(The antecedent of *his* is *each*.)

WRONG: Neither of the girls had remembered to bring their notebook.
RIGHT: Neither of the girls had remembered to bring *her* notebook.
(The antecedent of *her* is *neither*.)

WRONG: I asked everybody to do their best.
RIGHT: I asked everybody to do *his or her* best.
(The antecedent of *his or her* is *everybody*.)

WRONG: Did anybody do the work themselves?
RIGHT: Did anybody do the work *himself*?
(The antecedent of *himself* is *anybody*.)

WRONG: Mathematics has always interested me with their concrete yet abstract nature.
RIGHT: Mathematics has always interested me with *its* concrete yet abstract nature.
(The antecedent of *its* is *mathematics*.)

Exercise

Directions: Write a "C" on the line if the sentence is correct. Write an "X" on the line if there is an error in number agreement of a pronoun and its antecedent.

_____ 1. Every one of my girl friends has given their opinion of me.

_____ 2. Every person who asked was permitted to bring his or her book to class to use during the examination.

_____ 3. Neither the doctor nor her patients had an opportunity to express their feelings.

_____ 4. I am looking for a person who has forgotten their suitcase.

_____ 5. Each of the children may use the swimming pool if he promises to be careful.

_____ 6. Neither my sisters nor my mother has remembered her promise to me.

_____ 7. Many of the students explained his situation to me personally.

_____ 8. If anybody is in the office, they will answer their telephone.

_____ 9. If everybody who had come to the meeting had brought their report with them, the meeting would have gone a lot more smoothly.

_____ 10. Neither the cat nor the dogs will eat the food I bought for him.

_____ **11.** One of my daughters has left her purse on the coffee table.

_____ **12.** Neither of the police officers was willing to give me his name.

_____ **13.** The news from that country is well known for their objectivity.

_____ **14.** Either the boss or her workers will have to give a little of their time to solve this problem.

_____ **15.** Great works of art, such as the *Mona Lisa* and *Whistler's Mother*, can be deceptive in their simplicity.

_____ **16.** One sometimes gives up something they want for the sake of others.

_____ **17.** One of the first students to come into the room could not find his name on the list.

_____ **18.** Nobody lost their patience even though the meeting was long and boring.

_____ **19.** Everybody must pay their fair share towards the gift.

_____ **20.** All of my friends brought their husbands with them to my party.

Check your answers using the error key on page 96.

Those Modified

The demonstrative pronoun *those* can be followed by a phrase or clause that modifies it.

> CLAUSE
> No one is allowed in the room except *those who have paid*.

> PHRASE
> *Those waiting to see the doctor* may go in now.

> **Note**   The *personal* pronouns *they* and *them* should not be modified by a phrase or clause.

Error Examples

WRONG: They who need a receipt should sign here.
 RIGHT: *Those* who need a receipt should sign here.

WRONG: For them interested in learning, the university offers a good program.
 RIGHT: For *those* interested in learning, the university offers a good program.

WRONG: We invited only them we like to the party.
 RIGHT: We invited only *those* we like to the party.

Exercise

_____ 1.   She told her secret to only those she trusted.

_____ 2.   He will consider hiring only them currently studying art.

_____ 3.   The police turned the crowd away since only they with a permit could protest.

_____ 4.   Please send this pamphlet to those who have expressed an interest in this study.

_____ 5.   This line is for them with discount coupons.

_____ 6.   For them of you who appreciate good music, there is an excellent concert this evening.

_____ 7.   For them who like to travel to a warm place, Fiji is a paradise.

_____ 8.   The chairman of the board will talk to those whom he has already interviewed.

_____ 9.   Those who wish to bring their children to the party may do so.

_____ 10. They who arrive early will get the best selection of seats.

Check your answers using the error key on page 96.

Chapter Quiz

Directions: Write a "C" on the line if the sentence is correct. Write an "X" on the line if there is an error with the pronoun.

_____ 1. When one has many problems, he should try to solve them one at a time.

_____ 2. Mary could never understand him wanting to be a nurse.

_____ 3. I often think back to the time when mutual friends introduced Paul and I.

_____ 4. Claire noticed many people who had been waiting hours to buy their tickets.

_____ 5. When the children realized that they were by theirselves in the dark, they became really frightened.

_____ 6. In the course of life one should always remember their old friends.

_____ 7. Do you remember the teacher that his daughter became a doctor?

_____ 8. For them of you who wish to know more about journalism, we recommend that you order a book from the following list.

_____ 9. Neither my aunt nor my cousins were able to explain their behavior.

_____ 10. Mary was surprised to realize that it was us, her old school friends, calling her from Paris.

_____ 11. The dean asked all the students, including Betty and I, to show our visitor every possible courtesy.

_____ 12. Give the refunds to those who have filled out the correct form.

_____ 13. They say that English can be a very difficult language for one to learn in his later years.

_____ 14. Modern society, including conservatives, liberals, hippies, and blacks, has many problems that they must solve.

_____ 15. Elaine met the actress who you admire so much.

_____ 16. Bob called to his old friend John as he walked across the campus.

_____ 17. In the paper it says it is going to rain today.

_____ 18. Did you ever see a man as tall as he?

_____ 19. Neither of the girls remembered to give I her notebook.

_____ 20. I am worried about your having to review so much material.

Check your answers using the error key on page 97.

ERROR KEYS

(All references to rules and notes refer to the specific section where the quiz appears.)

Relative Pronouns

___X___ **1.** (novels *which* deal) OR (novels *that* deal). See rules 2 and 3.

___X___ **2.** (a man *whose* experience). See rule 4.

___C___ **3.**

___X___ **4.** (a dress *which*) OR (a dress *that*). See rules 2 and 3.

___C___ **5.**

___C___ **6.**

___X___ **7.** (a man *who*) OR (a man *that*). See rules 1 and 3.

___C___ **8.**

___X___ **9.** (the baby *who*) OR (the baby *that*). See rules 1 and 3.

___X___ **10.** (woman *whose* photograph). See rule 4.

Personal Pronouns—Case

___X___ **1.** (Betty and *he* were hurt). See rule 1.

___C___ **2.**

___X___ **3.** (by *himself*). See note c.

___X___ **4.** (Margaret and *me*). See rule 2 and note a.

___C___ **5.**

___X___ **6.** (of Susan and *her*). See rule 2.

___C___ **7.**

___C___ **8.**

___C___ **9.**

___X___ **10.** (my husband or *me*). See rule 2.

___X___ **11.** (by *themselves*). See note c.

___X___ **12.** (as intelligent as *he*). See note b.

___C___ **13.**

___C___ **14.**

___X___ **15.** (It is *she*). See rule 1.

WHO/WHOM

___X___ **1.** (*who* I thought were). See rules 1a and 2.

___X___ **2.** (*whom* you trust). See rule 1b.

___C___ **3.**

___X___ **4.** (*whom* I think you met). See rules 1b and 2.

___C___ **5.**

___X___ **6.** (*whom* the teacher chose). See rule 1b.

___C___ **7.**

___C___ **8.**

___X___ **9.** (*who* do you think will). See rules 1a and 2.

___C___ **10.**

___X___ **11.** (*who* handled). See rule 1a.

___X___ **12.** (to *whomever* you like). See rule 1b.

___X___ **13.** (*whoever* answers). See rule 1a.

___C___ **14.**

___X___ **15.** (*who* are working). See rule 1a.

Possessives

___C___ **1.**

___X___ **2.** (*your* saying good-bye)

___C___ **3.**

___C___ **4.**

___X___ **5.** (*their* leaving)

___X___ **6.** (*its* meowing). See note.

___X___ **7.** (*His* playing)

___C___ **8.**

___C___ **9.**

___X___ **10.** (*my* having to drive)

___C___ **11.**

___X___ **12.** (*his* winning)

___C___ **13.**

___X___ **14.** (*our* whispering)

___X___ **15.** (*my* taking)

Faulty Reference

____X____ 1. (*Mr. Smith* told Mr. Jones, "*I* have lost). See first error example.

____X____ 2. (*The telephone directory* says). See fifth error example.

____C____ 3.

____X____ 4. (As *Cathy* was driving home from work, *she* saw her friend.) See second error example.

____X____ 5. (*the picture* looked strange). See fourth error example.

____C____ 6.

____X____ 7. (and *the stock market* suffered). See fourth error example.

____C____ 8.

____X____ 9. (*The newspaper* says). See fifth error example.

____X____ 10. (and now *the A Team* is in first place). See third error example.

Person

____X____ 1. (*he* feels). See first error example and note a.

____C____ 2.

____X____ 3. (*one's* rent). See third error example.

____C____ 4.

____C____ 5.

____X____ 6. (*he* must). See first error example.

____X____ 7. (*one meets*) OR (*he meets*). See second error example and note a.

____C____ 8.

____C____ 9.

____X____ 10. (when *one finds oneself*). See second error example.

Number

____X____ 1. (*her* opinion). The antecedent of *her* is *one*. See rule 2.

____C____ 2.

____C____ 3.

____X____ 4. (*his* suitcase). The antecedent of *his* is *person*. See rule 1.

____C____ 5.

____C____ 6.

____X____ 7. (*their* situation). The antecedent of *their* is *many*. See rule 1.

____X____ 8. (*he* will answer *his* telephone) The antecedent of *he* and *his* is *anybody*. See rule 2.

____X____ 9. (*his* report with *him*). The antecedent of *his* and *him* is *everybody*. See rule 2.

____X____ 10. (for *them*). The antecedent of *them* is *dogs*. See rule 3.

____C____ 11.

____C____ 12.

____X____ 13. (for *its* objectivity). The antecedent of *its* is *news*. See rule 4.

____C____ 14.

____C____ 15.

____X____ 16. (*one* wants) OR (*he* wants). The antecedent of *one* or *he* is *one*. See rule 2.

____C____ 17.

____X____ 18. (*his* patience). The antecedent of *his* is *nobody*. See rule 2.

____X____ 19. (*his* fair share). The antecedent of *his* is *everybody*. See rule 2.

____C____ 20.

THOSE Modified

____C____ 1.

____X____ 2. (*those* currently studying art)

____X____ 3. (*those* with a permit)

____C____ 4.

____X____ 5. (*those* with discount coupons)

____X____ 6. (*those* of you who appreciate good music)

____X____ 7. (*those* who like to travel)

____C____ 8.

____C____ 9.

____X____ 10. (*Those* who arrive early)

Chapter Quiz

C **1.**

X **2.** (*his* wanting). See *Possessives*, page 95.

X **3.** (Paul and *me*). See *Personal Pronouns—Case*, page 96.

C **4.**

X **5.** (by *themselves*). See *Personal Pronouns—Case*, page 95.

X **6.** (*one's* old friends) OR (*his* old friends). See *Person*, page 96.

X **7.** (teacher *whose* daughter). See *Relatives*, page 95.

X **8.** (For *those* of you). See *Those Modified*, page 96.

C **9.**

X **10.** (it was *we*). See *Personal Pronouns—Case*, page 95.

X **11.** (including Betty and *me*). See *Personal Pronouns—Case*, page 95.

C **12.**

C **13.**

X **14.** (*it* must solve). See *Number*, page 96.

X **15.** (*whom* you admire). See *Who/Whom*, page 95.

X **16.** (As Bob walked across the campus, he called to his old friend John.). See *Faulty Reference*, page 96.

X **17.** (*The paper says*). See *Faulty Reference*, page 96.

C **18.**

X **19.** (to give *me*). See *Personal Pronouns—Case*, page 95.

C **20.**

Basic Patterns

6

Indirect Objects

Some verbs may be followed by two objects (an indirect object and a direct object). The following shows the patterns used when verbs take two objects.

1. Some verbs may use the following two patterns:

   I.O.   D.O.
   My father often gives *me* a *gift*.

   OR

   D.O. + TO + OBJ.
   My father often gives a *gift to me*.

   Some other verbs like *give* are: *bring, send, offer, pass, take, tell, read, write, teach,* and *sell*.

2. Some verbs may use the following two patterns:

   I.O.   D.O.
   John usually buys *Mary* a *gift*.

   OR

   D.O. + FOR + OBJ.
   John usually buys a *gift for Mary*.

   Some other verbs like *buy* are: *fix, make,* and *get*.

3. Some verbs use only the following pattern:

   D.O. + TO + OBJ.
   He explained his *idea to us*.

   Some other verbs like *explain* are: *announce, describe, deliver, mention, say, report,* and *return*.

4. Some verbs may use only the following pattern:

   I.O.   D.O.
   I asked *Mary* a *question*.

   Some other verbs like *ask* are: *cost* and *charge*.

Error Examples

WRONG: Susan's friend sent to her a beautiful silk dress from China.
 RIGHT: Susan's friend sent *her* a beautiful silk dress from China.

OR

Susan's friend sent a beautiful silk dress *to her* from China.

WRONG: John fixed the broken lamp to Harold.
 RIGHT: John fixed the broken lamp *for* Harold.

WRONG: The professor explained me the difficult point of grammar.
  RIGHT: The professor explained the difficult point of grammar *to me*.

WRONG: The new suit cost over forty dollars to me.
  RIGHT: The new suit cost *me* over forty dollars.

WRONG: The store charged over fifteen dollars to me to alter the jacket I bought.
  RIGHT: The store charged *me* over fifteen dollars to alter the jacket I bought.

Exercise

Directions: Write a "C" on the line if the sentence is correct. Write an "X" on the line if there is an indirect object error.

_____ **1.** We returned the defective merchandise to the store immediately.

_____ **2.** I hope you will write to me long letters while you are away.

_____ **3.** When do you think you can deliver them the package?

_____ **4.** That is the third time you have asked me the same question.

_____ **5.** My mother is making for Mary a new skirt.

_____ **6.** Please pass the potatoes to me after you take some.

_____ **7.** The belt buckle cost over ten dollars to Bob.

_____ **8.** He taught to me everything he knew.

_____ **9.** When she was abroad, Laura got several pairs of earrings for her mother.

_____ **10.** He sent me a beautiful letter from Spain.

Check your answers using the answer key on page 113.

Order of Adverbs

1. In general, place adverbs (or adverbial phrases) after the verb or after the object, if any. (Do not separate the subject from the verb or the verb from its object.)

The two patterns are

    a. **Subject + verb + adverb**

        S + VERB + ADV.
        He works here .

    b. **Subject + verb + object + adverb or adverbial phrase**

        He wants to eat soon.

        S + VERB + OBJ.   ADV. PHRASE
        We see them from *time to time* .

2. Some adverbs can come before a single-word verb or the main verb.

> ADV.   VERB
> He *promptly left* the room.

> ADV.   MAIN VERB
> He was *quickly escorted* from the room.

3. Single-word adverbs of frequency usually come after the verb *to be* and before a single-word verb or the main verb. (Note: Common adverbs of frequency are: *often*, *rarely*, *sometimes*, *frequently*, *occasionally*, *ever*, *never*, *seldom*, *usually*, and *always*.)

> BE ADV.
> He *is never* on time.

> ADV. VERB
> I *often see* her.

> ADV.   MAIN VERB
> I had *frequently noticed* her.

4. *Still* comes before a single-word verb or the main verb in affirmative sentences and before the auxiliary in negative sentences.

> MAIN VERB
> He is *still waiting* for you.

> AUX.
> He *still has* not answered my questions.

5. In general, the order of final adverbs is *place* and then *time*.

> PLACE   TIME
> He went to *Europe* last *summer*.

> PLACE   TIME
> I saw him at *the library last night*.

Error Examples

WRONG: John in the classroom is waiting.
RIGHT: John is waiting *in the classroom*.

WRONG: Betty is writing in her bedroom letters.
RIGHT: Betty is writing letters *in her bedroom*.

WRONG: Alex played with great passion the piano.
RIGHT: Alex played the piano *with great passion*.

WRONG: I write sometimes letters to my parents.
RIGHT: I *sometimes* write letters to my parents.

WRONG: John waited seldom for me.
RIGHT: John *seldom* waited for me.

WRONG: He rarely is on time.
RIGHT: He is *rarely* on time.

WRONG: Bob prepares once in a while dinner.
RIGHT: Bob prepares dinner *once in a while*.

WRONG: She bought yesterday several new dresses.
RIGHT: She bought several new dresses *yesterday*.

WRONG: They wrote during the summer to us.
RIGHT: They wrote to us *during the summer*.

WRONG: He sold immediately the gold watch.
RIGHT: He sold the gold watch *immediately*.

WRONG: He has read before that book.
RIGHT: He has read that book *before*.

WRONG: He is studying still in the library.
RIGHT: He is *still* studying in the library.

WRONG: They have not still finished.
RIGHT: They *still* have not finished.

WRONG: He sent his daughter in the summer to college.
RIGHT: He sent his daughter *to college in the summer*.

Exercise

Directions: Write a "C" on the line if the sentence is correct. Write an "X" on the line if there is an error in the placement of the adverb.

_____ **1.** He hopes to Rome to be able to go.

_____ **2.** The doctor sees patients only in the afternoon.

_____ **3.** David last evening went to the movies.

_____ **4.** He executed with verve the difficult piano passage.

_____ **5.** He found several useful books in my bookcase.

_____ **6.** He wants still to move to London next year.

_____ **7.** I observe frequently his behavior.

_____ **8.** He recently met with his new advisor.

_____ **9.** Tom lately has been working on his new book.

_____ **10.** He was suddenly amused by her spontaneity.

_____ **11.** He wrote usually in that unconventional style.

_____ **12.** They still do not appreciate their good luck.

_____ **13.** Jill during her college years lived in France.

_____ **14.** Has he seen the city before?

_____ **15.** Karl still has not remembered where he put his keys.

_____ **16.** The teacher posted on her office door her office hours.

_____ **17.** He is often accused of not being a serious person.

_____ **18.** Betty noticed rarely my hard work.

_____ **19.** John last night telephoned me.

_____ **20.** He went to the kitchen in the middle of the night for a glass of water.

Check your answers using the error key on page 113.

Embedded Questions

1. The pattern for an embedded question in a statement is *question word + subject + verb* or *question word/subject* (same word) + *verb*.

   QW   +   S + V
   I cannot see *what the sign says* .

   QW + S + V
   She does not know *where she should go* .

   QW/S + V
   They did not know *who bought the car* .

2. The pattern for an embedded question in a question is the same as for an embedded question in a statement. (See rule 1.)

   QW+ S + V
   Do you know *who he is* ?

   QW/S + V
   Did he say *who called* ?

3. Do not use *do*, *does*, or *did* as auxiliaries in these patterns.

Error Examples

WRONG: I did not understand what did they mean.
 RIGHT: I did not understand what *they meant*.

WRONG: Do you know where is John?
 RIGHT: Do you know where *John is*?

WRONG: I was surprised when he told me how much does he study every day.
 RIGHT: I was surprised when he told me how much *he studies* every day.

WRONG: He told me when was he free during the week.
 RIGHT: He told me when *he was* free during the week.

WRONG: Tell me where they do go after class every day.
 RIGHT: Tell me where *they go* after class every day.

Exercise

Directions: Write a "C" on the line if the sentence is correct. Write an "X" on the line if there is an error in the pattern for embedded questions.

_____ 1. I will ask how much do they sell for.

_____ 2. Did the professor tell you when is the next test?

_____ 3. I wonder when it is going to begin.

_____ 4. Forget about where we are going to play tennis as it is starting to rain.

_____ 5. Did you see what did he do?

_____ 6. Do you remember how much the tuition was?

_____ 7. Ask the operator what is the charge for a three-minute call to New York.

_____ 8. We don't know when will we see our friends again.

_____ 9. He forgot where he parked his car.

_____ 10. Would you please ask them where is the subway entrance.

_____ 11. He sent a telegram saying when he would arrive.

_____ 12. I forgot to ask him what time does the class begin.

_____ 13. Bill did not realize what time it was when I knocked on the door.

_____ 14. Can you tell us who that distinguished-looking gentleman is?

_____ 15. Ask Mr. Blake what does his daughter study at the university.

_____ 16. Can you be sure where will he be this Friday afternoon?

_____ 17. We should find out how hot is it in the summer before we decide to vacation there.

_____ 18. Can anyone explain why he had that terrible attitude?

_____ 19. We never found the village where were born our parents.

_____ 20. She does not know who did paint that beautiful mural.

Check your answers using the error key on page 113.

To/For (Purpose)

Patterns for expressing purpose:

1. *for* + noun phrase

   N PHRASE
   John went to California *for a rest*.

2. *to* + simple form of the verb (that is, the infinitive)

   TO + VERB
   John went to California *to ski*.

Error Examples

WRONG: She moved to New York for getting a better job.
 RIGHT: She moved to New York *to get* a better job.

OR

She moved to New York *for* a better job.

WRONG: They went to the country for having a vacation.
 RIGHT: They went to the country *for* a vacation.

OR

They went to the country *to have* a vacation.

WRONG: We used the projector for to show a movie.
 RIGHT: We used the projector *to show* a movie.

Exercise

Directions: Write a "C" on the line if the sentence is correct. Write an "X" on the line if there is a *to/for* (purpose) error.

_____ **1.** He went to the lecture for hearing about the latest agricultural techniques.

_____ **2.** They studied hard to pass the TOEFL.

_____ **3.** We saved money this year for to take a trip to Hong Kong.

_____ **4.** They bought that book for trying to learn Japanese.

_____ **5.** He is studying for a master's degree in marketing.

_____ **6.** I came to the United States for to visit my relatives.

_____ **7.** She is desperately looking for work.

_____ **8.** John went to the doctor's office for his yearly check-up.

_____ **9.** Let's go shopping this afternoon for finding some camping equipment for our trip.

_____ **10.** Susan went to the printer's office to order some wedding invitations.

Check your answers using the error key on page 114.

Double Subjects

Do not use a noun and a pronoun as a subject. Only one is necessary.

       s
He saw my uncle the other day.

          s
The *woman* in the red dress is my teacher.

       s
It is easy to see from here.

Error Examples

WRONG: My brother he is always borrowing my car.
 RIGHT: My *brother is* always borrowing my car.

WRONG: Their method of teaching it is very good.
 RIGHT: Their method of *teaching is* very good.

WRONG: I could not believe that my boyfriend he told me a lie.
 RIGHT: I could not believe that my *boyfriend told* me a lie.

Exercise

Directions: Write a "C" on the line if the sentence is correct. Write an "X" on the line if there is a double-subject error.

_____   **1.** That subject it has always been difficult for me.

_____   **2.** I could not believe it when my boss gave me a raise.

_____   **3.** That is the man who he told me the bad news.

_____   **4.** They told me that their uncle was arriving this afternoon.

_____   **5.** You and I we always have a good time together.

_____   **6.** The TOEFL test it is a real challenge.

_____   **7.** That lobster is delicious because it is so fresh.

_____   **8.** Carol said that she and her sister they had bought a new car.

_____   **9.** The president was acquitted in the scandal.

_____   **10.** Your husband had a good excuse for arriving late.

Check your answers with the error key on page 114.

Clauses

Independent Clauses

1. Every sentence must have at least one independent clause. An independent clause consists of at least one subject and one finite verb (see note c) and is a complete thought. The following are examples of independent clauses:

   The *president* spoke.
   (s) (v)

   Betty made some iced tea.
   (s) (v)

   He is a doctor.
   (s) (v)

   They arrived at 2:00.
   (s) (v)

   I was there.
   (s) (v)

2. Two independent clauses can be joined by *and, but, or, nor,* or *for.*

   He went to the bank, *but it was* closed.
   (s) (v)   (s) (v)

   She had never *been* to Los Angeles before, *and she was* quite surprised at the rush-hour traffic jams.
   (s) (v)   (s) (v)

Dependent Clauses

3. A sentence may have one or more dependent clauses, each one of which must have its own subject and finite verb. A dependent clause must be attached to an independent clause. It is incomplete by itself. There are three kinds of dependent clauses: noun, relative (adjective), and adverb.

   A **noun clause** functions as a subject or an object. Each noun clause, which has its own subject and verb, may be an embedded statement or an embedded question.

   - Embedded statements are often introduced by *that.*

     That he was a criminal surprised me. *(N cl. as obj.)*
         (s) (v)

     I know *(that) he is* from Canada. *(N cl. as obj.)*
            (s) (v)

   - Embedded questions are introduced by *wh-* words.

     I do not know *what time the party begins.* *(N cl. as obj.)*
                              (s) (v)

     He talked about what *he had learned* in his class. *(N cl. as obj. of prep.)*
                          (s) (v)

A ***relative clause*** functions as an adjective. Each relative clause, which has its own subject and verb, is introduced by one of the following words: *who, whom, which, that,* and *whose.*

I do not know the lady *who lives next door.*
<small>s   v</small>

He is a man *(whom)* I respect.*
<small>s   v</small>

That is a fern plant, *which* never *blooms.*
<small>s   v</small>

This is the book *(that)* I borrowed from John.*
<small>s   v</small>

That is the couple *whose house burned down.*
<small>s   v</small>

An ***adverb clause*** functions as an adverb. Each adverb clause has its own subject and verb. The following is a list of commonly used words that introduce adverb clauses: *before, after, because, since, while, when, if,* and *although.* Introductory adverb clauses are followed by a comma.

Before she left, I told her.
<small>s   v</small>

When it began to rain, we left.
<small>s   v</small>

If I have time, I will help you.
<small>s   v</small>

Although he tried hard, he did not win the race.
<small>s   v</small>

We talked to her *after she had surgery.*
<small>s   v</small>

He did not go in *because he was late.*
<small>s   v</small>

I have not seen him *since he arrived.*
<small>s   v</small>

They met him *when they were at college.*
<small>s   v</small>

Notes   a. Be sure that every dependent clause is attached to an independent clause.

b. Remember that all clauses, independent and dependent, have their own subject and finite verb.

c. A finite verb is one that can be conjugated and shows tense, that is, ends in *-ed, -s,* etc. A gerund (V + *ing*) or an infinitive (*to* + V) is not a finite verb.

d. In this grammar explanation, when any word appears in parenthesis, it is optional in the sentence.

e. Remember that two independent clauses are joined by coordinate conjunctions (*and, but,* etc.). They cannot be joined by a comma only.

---

*Note: *Whom* and *that,* when used as objects, are optional.

Error Examples

WRONG: Give my regards to everyone asks about me.
 RIGHT: Give my regards to everyone *who* asks about me.

WRONG: Thinking for many centuries that the world was flat.
 RIGHT: *It was thought* for many centuries that the world was flat.

WRONG: President Kennedy committed the U.S. to being first to land men on the moon, he died before he saw his dream realized.
 RIGHT: President Kennedy committed the U.S. to being first to land men on the moon, *but* he died before he saw his dream realized.

WRONG: To believe that smoking causes some forms of cancer.
 RIGHT: *It is believed* that smoking causes some forms of cancer.

WRONG: That Mt. Everest is the highest peak in the world.
 RIGHT: *I know that* Mt. Everest is the highest peak in the world.

OR

Mt. Everest is the highest peak in the world.

WRONG: Because I did not have enough money to go on vacation this year.
 RIGHT: Because I did not have enough money to go on vacation this year, *I stayed home*.

OR

I did not have enough money to go on vacation this year.

WRONG: We were surprised when saw her.
 RIGHT: We were surprised when *we saw* her.

WRONG: Where they would be staying in Greece.
 RIGHT: *She told me* where they would be staying in Greece.

Exercise

Directions: Write a "C" on the line if the sentence is correct. Write an "X" on the line if there is a clause error.

_____ 1. It is hoped that man will someday inhabit other planets.

_____ 2. Learning that the university plans to construct a new sports arena next year.

_____ 3. Since it was cool and overcast, we canceled the picnic.

_____ 4. Why he quit his job with that prestigious company.

_____ 5. Some people consider marriage to be the most important thing could happen in life.

_____ 6. That Columbus was not the first man to set foot in the New World.

_____ 7. He found the book he had been looking for under the sofa.

_____ 8. We went to San Diego, we spent many happy hours on the beach.

_____ 9. To think that everyone needs some form of physical exercise.

_____ 10. The store had a huge end-of-summer sale, and hundreds of people were at the door when it opened.

_____ 11. If any questions, please ask me for help.

_____ 12. That he survived that terrible accident surprised everyone who heard the news.

_____ 13. There is the artist whose painting received an award.

_____ 14. She is the only person in this country knows how to operate that new equipment.

_____ 15. I noticed that the new couple next door not at home last week.

Check your answers using the error key on page 114.

CHAPTER QUIZ
Error Identification

Directions: For the Error Identification questions, each sentence contains four underlined words or phrases. Select the one word or phrase that must be changed in order for the sentence to be correct. Circle your answer in the book or mark your answer on a separate sheet of paper.

1. I did not understand their predicament until John explained me all the details of the mishap.
   (A)   (B)   (C)   (D)

2. Even though we had been to her house several times before, we did not remember exactly what
   (A)   (B)   (C)
   street was it on.
   (D)

3. We are never happy with what we have in life; the grass always is greener on the other side of the fence.
   (A)   (B)   (C)   (D)

4. The opera, even though performed by amateurs, it was excellent.
   (A)   (B)   (C)(D)

5. Because of their countries' great need for expertise in computer programming, the students
   (A)   (B)
   were sent for studying in the United States.
   (C)   (D)

6. Mr. Shimoto was planning to send to me a package from Japan as soon as he arrived home from
   (A) (B)   (C)   (D)
   his trip to Hawaii.

7. I was surprised to hear that the store charged Dr. Brown an extra amount when it delivered
   (A)   (B)   (C)
   to his office his new sofa.
   (D)

8. When John asked Tomoko, the Japanese student, what she did think of the museum, she quickly
   (A)   (B)
   replied that it had taught her a great deal about the history of the area.
   (C)   (D)

9. His father mentioned to me that Robert had written to him requesting money for buying a new car.
   (A)   (B) (C)   (D)

10. The author of this new book she is planning to write a sequel in order to capitalize on the
    (A)   (B)   (C)
    publicity she has received recently.
    (D)

Check your answers using the error key on page 114.

Sentence Completion

Directions: In the Sentence Completion questions, one or more words are left out of each sentence. Under each sentence, you will see four words or phrases. Select the one word or phrase that completes the sentence correctly, then write it in the space provided in the book or on a separate sheet of paper.

1. _____ is indispensable to the economy of that region.

   (A) That copper mining
   (B) It is copper mining
   (C) Although copper mining
   (D) Copper mining

2. She read _____.

   (A) several chapters in the library last night
   (B) last night several chapters in the library
   (C) last night in the library several chapters
   (D) in the library several chapters last night

3. Doris went to the nicest store in the city _____ presents for her children.

   (A) for to get
   (B) for getting
   (C) to get
   (D) to getting

4. The man on the horse _____ a famous movie star.

   (A) he is
   (B) is he
   (C) who is
   (D) is

5. Please do not ever mention _____.

   (A) that subject again to us
   (B) that subject to us again
   (C) to us that subject again
   (D) again to us that subject

6. She cannot remember where _____ her black jacket.

   (A) did she leave
   (B) she did leave
   (C) she left
   (D) left she

7. The doctor explained _____ that we should have a complete physical examination once a year.

   (A) us
   (B) for us
   (C) to us
   (D) at us

8. Would you please tell us _____.

   (A) when the next bus comes
   (B) when comes the next bus
   (C) when does the next bus come
   (D) when the next bus does come

9. That attractive man _____ my cousin who is visiting us from France.

   (A) who is
   (B) he is
   (C) is
   (D) is he

10. They _____ to our proposal.

   (A) have not still responded
   (B) have not responded still
   (C) have still not responded
   (D) still have not responded

Check your answers using the error key on page 114.

ERROR KEYS

(All references to rules and notes refer to the specific section where the quiz appears.)

Indirect Objects

__C__ **1.**

__X__ **2.** (*write me* long letters) OR (write long letters *to me*). See rule 1.

__X__ **3.** (deliver the package *to them*). See rule 3.

__C__ **4.**

__X__ **5.** (is *making Mary* a new skirt) OR (is making a new skirt *for Mary*). See rule 2.

__C__ **6.**

__X__ **7.** (*cost Bob* over ten dollars). See rule 4.

__X__ **8.** (*taught me* everything) OR (taught everything he knew *to me*). See rule 1.

__C__ **9.**

__C__ **10.**

Order of Adverbs

__X__ **1.** (He hopes to be able to go *to Rome*.) See rule 1, pattern 1a.

__C__ **2.**

__X__ **3.** (David went to the movies *last evening*.) See rule 1, pattern 1a and rule 5.

__X__ **4.** (He executed the difficult piano passage *with verve*.) See rule 1, pattern 1b.

__C__ **5.**

__X__ **6.** (He *still* wants). See rule 4.

__X__ **7.** (I *frequently* observe.) See rule 3.

__C__ **8.**

__X__ **9.** (Tom has been working on his new book *lately*.) See rule 1, pattern 1b.

__C__ **10.**

__X__ **11.** (He *usually* wrote). See rule 3.

__C__ **12.**

__X__ **13.** (Jill lived in France *during her college years*.) See rule 1, pattern 1a, and rule 5.

__C__ **14.**

__C__ **15.**

__X__ **16.** (The teacher posted her office hours *on her office door*.) See rule 1, pattern 1b.

__C__ **17.**

__X__ **18.** (Betty *rarely* noticed my hard work.) See rule 3.

__X__ **19.** (John telephoned me *last night*.) See rule 1, pattern 1b.

__C__ **20.**

Embedded Questions

__X__ **1.** (*how much they sell for*). See rule 3.

__X__ **2.** (*when the next test is?*). See rule 2.

__C__ **3.**

__C__ **4.**

__X__ **5.** (*what he did?*). See rule 3.

__C__ **6.**

__X__ **7.** (*what the charge is*). See rule 1.

__X__ **8.** (*when we will see*). See rule 1.

__C__ **9.**

__X__ **10.** (*where the subway entrance is*). See rule 1.

__C__ **11.**

__X__ **12.** (*what time the class begins*). See rule 3.

__C__ **13.**

__C__ **14.**

__X__ **15.** (*what his daughter studies*). See rule 3.

__X__ **16.** (*where he will be*). See rule 2.

__X__ **17.** (*how hot it is*). See rule 1.

__C__ **18.**

__X__ **19.** (*where our parents were born*). See rule 1.

__X__ **20.** (*who painted*). See rule 3.

TO/FOR (Purpose)

<u> X </u> **1.** (*to hear*). See rule 2.

<u> C </u> **2.**

<u> X </u> **3.** (year *to take* a trip) OR (year *for a trip*). See rules 1 and 2.

<u> X </u> **4.** (book *to try* to learn). See rule 2.

<u> C </u> **5.**

<u> X </u> **6.** (United States *to visit*). See rule 2.

<u> C </u> **7.**

<u> C </u> **8.**

<u> X </u> **9.** (*to find*). See rule 2.

<u> C </u> **10.**

Double Subjects

<u> X </u> **1.** (*subject has* always)

<u> C </u> **2.**

<u> X </u> **3.** (*who told* me)

<u> C </u> **4.**

<u> X </u> **5.** (*You and I always*) OR (*We always*)

<u> X </u> **6.** (*test is* a real)

<u> C </u> **7.**

<u> X </u> **8.** (she and her *sister had bought*)

<u> C </u> **9.**

<u> C </u> **10.**

Clauses

<u> C </u> **1.**

<u> X </u> **2.** (*It was learned* that). See rule 3 and note b.

<u> C </u> **3.**

<u> X </u> **4.** (*I cannot understand why* he quit his job.). See rule 3, (**noun clause**) and note a.

<u> X </u> **5.** (thing *that* could). See rule 3, (**relative clause**) and note b.

<u> X </u> **6.** (*Columbus was not the first man to set foot in the New World* OR *That Columbus was not the first man to set foot in the New World is not surprising.*) See rule 3 (**noun clause**) and note a.

<u> C </u> **7.**

<u> X </u> **8.** (Diego, *and* we spent). See rule 2 and note d.

<u> X </u> **9.** (*It is thought that*). See rule 3 and notes b and c.

<u> C </u> **10.**

<u> X </u> **11.** (If *you have* any). See rule 3, (**adverb clause**) and note b.

<u> C </u> **12.**

<u> C </u> **13.**

<u> X </u> **14.** (country *who* knows). See rule 3, (**relative clause**) and note b.

<u> X </u> **15.** (door *was* not). See rule 3 and note b.

Chapter Quiz

Error Identification

<u> (C) </u> **1.** See *Indirect Objects*, page 113.

<u> (D) </u> **2.** See *Embedded Questions*, page 113.

<u> (C) </u> **3.** See *Order of Adverbs*, page 113.

<u> (C) </u> **4.** See *Double Subjects*, page 114.

<u> (D) </u> **5.** See *To/For(Purpose)*, page 114.

<u> (B) </u> **6.** See *Indirect Objects*, page 113.

<u> (D) </u> **7.** See *Order of Adverbs*, page 113.

<u> (A) </u> **8.** See *Embedded Questions*, page 113.

<u> (D) </u> **9.** See *To/For (Purpose)*, page 114.

<u> (A) </u> **10.** See *Double Subjects*, page 114.

Sentence Completion

<u> (D) </u> **1.** See *Clauses*, page 114.

<u> (A) </u> **2.** See *Order of Adverbs*, page 113.

<u> (C) </u> **3.** See *To/For (Purpose)*, page 114.

<u> (D) </u> **4.** See *Double Subjects*, page 114.

<u> (B) </u> **5.** See *Order of Adverbs*, page 113.

<u> (C) </u> **6.** See *Embedded Questions*, page 113.

<u> (C) </u> **7.** See *Indirect Objects*, page 113.

<u> (A) </u> **8.** See *Embedded Questions*, page 113.

<u> (C) </u> **9.** See *Double Subjects*, page 114.

<u> (D) </u> **10.** See *Order of Adverbs*, page 113.

Style

Voice

In English, the active voice is more common than the passive voice, although the passive voice is acceptable and even preferred at times.

1. The passive voice is preferred when the actor is unknown or unimportant.

    > PASSIVE
    > The cure for cancer *will* probably *be discovered* by some unknown scientist in a laboratory.
    > PASSIVE
    > That church *was built* in 1549. (*Who* built the church is unimportant and not mentioned.)

2. The passive voice is often used when discussing history.

    > PASSIVE
    > The war *was fought* over gold.

3. Use the active voice when the actor is more important than the action.

    > ACTORS ACTIVE
    > The *children ate* spaghetti for dinner.

    > ACTORS ACTIVE
    > *We watched* the news.

4. Avoid using active and passive in the same sentence if possible.

    > PASSIVE   PASSIVE
    > The flowers *were planted* and the trees *were trimmed*.

    > ACTIVE   ACTIVE
    > Susan *cooked* the dinner and *washed* the dishes.

5. Use one verb instead of two when possible.

    > Rita enjoys good food and music. **Not:** Rita enjoys good food and music is also enjoyed by her.

Error Examples

In the following examples, we cannot say that the first sentence is absolutely *wrong*. In certain contexts, it may even be preferred. However, generally speaking, the corrected sentence (the second sentence) is preferable. We are calling the first sentence AWKWARD and the second sentence BETTER.

AWKWARD: Ice cream was eaten at the party by the children.
  BETTER: The children ate ice cream at the party.

AWKWARD: Workers built the pyramids about 5,000 years ago.
  BETTER: The pyramids were built about 5,000 years ago.

AWKWARD: Some people painted pictures of animals on ancient cave walls.
BETTER: Pictures of animals were painted on ancient cave walls.

AWKWARD: The house was bought by my mother and father in 1970.
BETTER: My mother and father bought the house in 1970.

AWKWARD: Henry likes swimming and golfing is also liked by him.
BETTER: Henry likes swimming and golfing.

AWKWARD: Sally loves children and her summers are spent working in a summer camp.
BETTER: Sally loves children and spends her summers working in a summer camp.

AWKWARD: The rainbow was seen by us as the storm began to subside.
BETTER: We saw the rainbow as the storm began to subside.

Exercise

Directions: Write a "C" on the line if the sentence seems correct as written. Write an "A" (for awkward) on the line if the choice of voice seems incorrect.

_____   **1.** Steak was eaten by me last night.

_____   **2.** When we work hard, we accomplish a lot.

_____   **3.** Jane wrote a very good composition for her writing class.

_____   **4.** We laughed when the clown fell out of the car.

_____   **5.** Workers built the road in two years at a cost of five million dollars.

_____   **6.** The people loved their leader and his mistakes were forgiven by them.

_____   **7.** The phone was answered by John on the first ring.

_____   **8.** Paul teaches English in high school and writes short stories in his free time.

_____   **9.** Most American cars are built in Detroit, Michigan.

_____ **10.** My uncle worked hard all his life and left a sizable estate when he died.

_____ **11.** My father and I played chess for several hours yesterday.

_____ **12.** As we neared the house, a small dog sitting on the porch could be seen by us.

_____ **13.** Some people committed a lot of crimes in this neighborhood last month.

_____ **14.** If you studied more, your tests could be easily passed.

_____ **15.** The students opened their books and began to read.

_____ **16.** As John approaches his fortieth birthday, he is reassessing the direction of his life.

_____ **17.** The light was turned on by me as I entered my bedroom.

_____ **18.** That electronics company is expanding, and many new products are being developed by them.

_____ **19.** Soldiers fought the Battle of Hastings in 1066.

_____ **20.** Her earrings were put on by Jane before she went to the party.

_____ **21.** During the war thousands of persons were forced to leave their homes.

_____ **22.** Claire painted the living room, and a new carpet was laid by her.

_____ **23.** Jack works hard during the week and his free time is spent sailing his new boat.

_____ **24.** The students were carefully selected and they represented the class well.

_____ **25.** Bob plays the piano and, the guitar is played by him also.

Check your answers using the error key on page 157.

Parallelism

1. Items in a series must be parallel; that is, they must have the same grammatical form.

Nouns

N   N   N
He likes *music*, *art*, and *history*.

Gerunds

V + ING   V + ING   V + ING
swimming, *dancing*, and horseback *riding*.

Adjectives

ADJ. ADJ.   ADJ.
He is *tall*, *dark*, and *handsome*.

Infinitives

INFIN.   INFIN.   INFIN.
They wanted *to paint* the living room, *to lay* a new carpet, and *to buy* a new sofa.

Note The preposition *to* may be omitted in the second and third infinitives.

Past Tense

PAST   PAST   PAST
The Romans *conquered*, *colonized*, and *governed* much of the world.

Past Perfect Tense

PAST PERF.   PAST PERF.   PAST PERF.
He *had finished* the game, *had taken* a shower, and *had eaten* lunch by the time I got to his house.

Note The auxiliary *had* may be omitted in the second and third verb phrases.

2. Structures joined by *and*, *but*, *as*, *or*, *than*, or *although* must have the same grammatical form.

And

N PHRASE   N PHRASE

He enjoyed *the music of Spain* <u>*and*</u> *the sculpture of France*.

But

ADJ.   ADJ.

That verb form is not *active*, <u>*but*</u> *passive*.

As

V + ING   V + ING

Taking the bus can be as costly <u>*as*</u> *taking* a plane.

Or

INFIN.   INFIN.

He wanted *to borrow* a car <u>*or*</u> *to rent* one while his car was being repaired.

Than

V + ING   V + ING

Eating in a restaurant is more fun <u>*than*</u> *cooking* at home.

Although

INFIN.   INFIN.

<u>*Although*</u> he liked *to eat* good food, he did not like *to pay* high prices for it.

Error Examples

WRONG: When they were in Mexico, they saw museums, ruins, and folk dancing.
  RIGHT: When they were in Mexico, they saw museums, ruins, and folk *dances*.

WRONG: He is young, intelligent, and has charm.
  RIGHT: He is young, intelligent, and *charming*.

WRONG: She likes to read, to travel, and painting.
  RIGHT: She likes to read, to travel, and *to paint*.

WRONG: They came out of the building hurriedly, hailed a cab, and jump into it.
  RIGHT: They came out of the building hurriedly, hailed a cab, and *jumped* into it.

WRONG: Her husband had bought a house, found a job, and chose a school for the children before
          she arrived.
  RIGHT: Her husband had bought a house, found a job, and *chosen* a school for the children
          before she arrived.

WRONG: We enjoyed the varied cuisine and going to the excellent theater in New York.
  RIGHT: We enjoyed the varied cuisine and *the excellent theater* in New York.

WRONG: That soup should not be served hot, but at a cold temperature.
  RIGHT: That soup should not be served hot, but *cold*.

WRONG: Renting an apartment can be as expensive as to buy a house.
  RIGHT: Renting an apartment can be as expensive as *buying* a house.

WRONG: He did not like to swim or skiing.

RIGHT: He did not like to swim or *to ski*.

WRONG: Going on vacation is more fun than to work in the summer.

RIGHT: Going on vacation is more fun than *working* in the summer.

Exercise

Directions: Write a "C" on the line if the sentence is correct. Write an "X" on the line if there is an error in parallelism.

_____ **1.** When he was a college student, he learned to play tennis, to golf, and swimming.

_____ **2.** Do not speak out, but raise your hand.

_____ **3.** To face adversity, to solve problems, and to overcome difficulties all give one a sense of satisfaction.

_____ **4.** We enjoyed the perfect weather and seeing fjords in Norway.

_____ **5.** Go to Window A, ask for a form, and bring it back to me.

_____ **6.** Before he died, he had sold his house, wrote a will, and set up a trust fund.

_____ **7.** Her hobbies are reading, playing the piano, and gardening.

_____ **8.** Being a homemaker is as difficult as working in an office.

_____ **9.** After years of dealing with the public, she developed great charm, wit, and confident.

_____ **10.** On their vacation they enjoyed swimming at the beach, walking through the quaint streets, and sitting in the picturesque parks.

_____ **11.** He could not decide whether to get a job or studying.

_____ **12.** Although he was quick to criticize, he was slow praising his students.

_____ **13.** The presidential candidate was a man of intellectual strength, moral character, and personal integrity.

_____ **14.** The bellhop took my bags to my room, opened the door, and puts them at the foot of the bed.

_____ **15.** Jogging is more vigorous exercise than to play golf.

Check your answers using the error key on page 157.

Wordiness

A general rule in English might be that "shorter is better." That is, when the same idea can be expressed directly in fewer words, choose the shorter version. There are several ways to do this:

1. Avoid unnecessary passive constructions. See *Voice* on page 115 of this chapter.

2. Avoid unnecessary relative clauses where an adjective, participal phrase, prepositional phrase, or appositive is enough.

   ADJ.
   The *tall* man bought the car.

   Not: The man *who is tall* bought the car.

   PART. PHRASE
   The young girl *waiting by the door* would like to see you.

   Not: The young girl *who is waiting by the door* would like to see you.

   PREP. PHRASE
   The package *on the table* is ready to be mailed.

   Not: The package *that is on the table* is ready to be mailed.

   APPOSITIVE
   Hawaii, *the fiftieth state*, is a favorite vacation spot.

   Not: Hawaii, *which is the fiftieth* state, is a favorite vacation spot.

3. Be as direct as possible.

   It was an important discovery.

   Not: It was a discovery *of great importance*.

   He noticed a pretty girl.

   Not: He noticed *a girl who was pretty*.

   She did enzyme research from 1950 to 1964.

   Not: She spent *a total of fourteen years,* from 1950 to 1964, *in the research area of enzymes*.

   He walked down the stairs quickly.

   Not: He walked down the stairs *in a quick manner*.

4. Avoid redundancy (repetition of the same idea).

   She returned on Monday.

   Not: She returned *back* on Monday.

   His virtue was well known.

   Not: His virtue *and goodness* were well known. (*Virtue* is *goodness*.)

Error Examples

In the following examples, we cannot say that the first sentence is absolutely *wrong*. However, generally speaking, the corrected sentence (the second sentence) is preferable. We are calling the first sentence WEAK and the second sentence PREFERRED.

     WEAK: The examination was finished by all the students within the allocated time.
PREFERRED: All the students finished the examination in time.

     WEAK: The professor, who was tall and blond, lectured about medieval architecture.
PREFERRED: The *tall, blond* professor lectured about medieval architecture.

     WEAK: Paul read Jane's letter in an excited state of mind
PREFERRED: Paul *excitedly* read Jane's letter.

WEAK: The committee discussed the problem for a long time without being able to come to the point where a decision could be reached.
PREFERRED: The committee discussed the problem for a long time *without reaching a decision.*

WEAK: Crime and illegal acts are on the rise.
PREFERRED: *Crime* is on the rise. (*Crime* is *illegal acts.*)

WEAK: The girl who was wearing the colorful bathing suit is my cousin.
PREFERRED: The girl *wearing the colorful bathing suit* is my cousin.

WEAK: The glass figurine that was on display in the store window appealed to me.
PREFERRED: The glass figurine *on display in the store window* appealed to me.

WEAK: Boston, which is the capital of Massachusetts, has many universities and colleges.
PREFERRED: Boston, *the capital of Massachusetts*, has many universities and colleges.

Exercise

Directions: Write a "C" on the line if the sentence seems correct as written. Write a "W" on the line if the sentence seems *wordy* (to have too many words).

_____ **1,** The man indicated a negative response by shaking his head.

_____ **2.** The house will probably be finished in four months.

_____ **3.** The house on the corner burned down last night.

_____ **4.** Jane went to the store with the purpose of selecting and purchasing a new dress.

_____ **5.** Running on foot through the street, the thief was apprehended by the police.

_____ **6.** My wife and I argued for hours before deciding to send our son to summer camp.

_____ **7.** Bob saw several pieces of art that were expensive.

_____ **8.** Jenny received several speeding tickets.

_____ **9.** The ballerina danced her dances for hours.

_____ **10.** Professor Blanton, who is the college president, will speak on this topic.

_____ **11.** Betty opened the mysterious package cautiously.

_____ **12.** The saleswoman in the red dress insulted me.

_____ **13.** Three hours was the length of time that we found necessary to drive to New York.

_____ **14.** The Louvre, a world-famous art museum, is in Paris, France.

_____ **15.** The book was read by me in four hours.

Check your answers using the error key on page 157.

Substandard

Some words or phrases are *not* acceptable as correctly spoken English.

1. *Ain't* should not be used as a negative form of *to be*.

   John *is not* here.

   I *am not* ready.

   They *are not* coming.

2. Anywheres, nowheres, everywheres, and somewheres are incorrect forms of anywhere, nowhere, everywhere, and somewhere.

   I cannot find him *anywhere*.

   Mary put her purse *somewhere*.

3. *Alright* is an incorrect form of *all right*.

   Do you feel *all right*?

4. *Kind of a* and *sort of a* are incorrect forms of *kind of* and *sort of*. (In other words, the *a* is unnecessary and incorrect.)

   That is a *kind of* plant that grows in Africa.

   John is the *sort of* man who worries about other people.

5. *Mad* should not be used to mean *angry* when it precedes the preposition "with."

   The teacher was very *angry* with John.

6. *Off of* is an incorrect form of *off*.

   The couple stepped *off* the bus.

7. *Suspicion* is a noun and cannot be used as a verb. The correct verb form is *suspect*.

   Mary *suspects* that her assistant may be stealing from her.

8. *The reason is because* is an incorrect form of *the reason is that*.

   The reason that John cannot attend the meeting *is that* he is sick.

9. *Is where* and *is when* are incorrect ways of defining the meaning of a word.

   "To imitate" means "to act the same way as someone else."

   A "cookout" is "an outdoor party where food is generally cooked over charcoals."

10. *Different than* is an incorrect form of *different from*.

    John is *different from* his father.

Error Examples

WRONG: Betty ain't a good student.
 RIGHT: Betty *is not* a good student.

WRONG: The doctor looked everywheres for his prescription pad.
 RIGHT: The doctor looked *everywhere* for his prescription pad.

WRONG: The party was not wonderful, but at least the food was alright.
 RIGHT: The party was not wonderful, but at least the food was *all right*.

WRONG: That was the strangest kind of an animal that Harry had ever seen.
 RIGHT: That was the strangest *kind of* animal that Harry had ever seen.

WRONG: Sometimes a father can get very mad at his children.
 RIGHT: Sometimes a father can get very *angry with* his children.

WRONG: We try not to get off of the subject.
 RIGHT: We try not to get *off* the subject.

WRONG: The police suspicion that a local resident committed the crime.
 RIGHT: The police *suspect* that a local resident committed the crime.

WRONG: The reason that Mary is so upset is because she lost her wallet.
 RIGHT: *The reason* that Mary is so upset *is that* she lost her wallet.

WRONG: To "hyperventilate" is when one breathes too fast or too deeply.
 RIGHT: To "hyperventilate" is to "breathe too fast or too deeply."

WRONG: California is different than Arizona.
 RIGHT: California is *different from* Arizona.

Exercise

Directions: Write a "C" on the line if the sentence is correct. Write an "X" on the line if substandard (unacceptable, incorrect) English is used.

_____ **1.** Most situations turn out all right in the long run.

_____ **2.** Gerald explained that the reason he was late was because he had had car trouble.

_____ **3.** A "loan-word" is "a word that has come from another language."

_____ **4.** The Smiths bought a kind of a car that gets good mileage.

_____ **5.** "Parallel" is when objects are an equal distance apart at every point.

_____ **6.** The vase was made of a sort of material found only in Australia.

_____ **7.** The children were nowheres to be found.

_____ **8.** Henry took the picture off the wall and put it away.

_____ **9.** It looked like a terrible accident, but everyone in the car was alright.

_____ **10.** I believe the reason he left college was that he ran out of money.

_____ **11.** The Browns ain't coming to the church meeting tonight.

_____ **12.** I hope you do not suspicion that I cheated on the exam.

_____ **13.** A "knock-out" is where a person is rendered unconscious by a blow.

_____ **14.** The man acted so strangely that his family thought he was mad.

_____ **15.** Good and bad people can be found anywheres in the world.

_____ **16.** Do you find the United States much different than your country?

_____ **17.** The pen rolled off of the table and onto the floor.

_____ **18.** What sort of coat was the customer looking for?

_____ **19.** When John saw his grades, he felt very mad at his professor.

_____ **20.** What kind of a person could do a thing like this!

Check your answers with the error key on page 158.

Usage

Some words have similar meanings, but cannot be used interchangeably; that is, a choice must be made according to the grammatical situation.

1. **Between/Among**

    Between is used with *two* persons or things.

    I cannot decide *between* these two blouses.

    Among is used for *three or more* persons or things.

    He was standing *among* several students.

2. **Amount/Number**

    Amount is used with *non-count nouns*.

    He has a large *amount* of *money*.

    Number is used with *count nouns*.

    She has a large *number* of *children*.

3. **In/Into**

    In is used with *non-motion* verbs.

    He *is waiting in* the kitchen.

    Into is used with verbs of *motion*.

    He *ran into* the kitchen.

4. **Sit/Set**

    Sit cannot take an object. *Sit* tells what a person or thing does for himself or by itself. The principal parts of *sit* are:

sit (simple form)	He *sits* by the window.
sat (past form)	Bob *sat* in his room and read.
sat (past participle)	The guests have already *sat* down.
sitting (present participle)	The vase is *sitting* on the table.

    Set must have an object. *Set* tells what a person does for someone or something else. The principal parts of *set* are:

set (simple form)	Do not *set* your *glass* on the piano.
set (past form)	She *set* her *purse* on the floor last night.
set (past participle)	Have you *set* the *table* yet?
setting (present participle)	*Setting* the *vase* on the coffee table, Mary noticed that the vase had a crack in it.

5. **Lie/Lay**

Lie cannot take an object. *Lie* tells what a person or thing does for himself or by itself. The principal parts of *lie* are:

lie (simple form)	John *lies* on his bed for a few minutes after lunch every day.
lay (past form)	Mary *lay* on the sofa all yesterday afternoon.
lain (past participle)	The watch had *lain* unnoticed for several days before I found it.
lying (present participle)	A man was *lying* injured in the street after the accident.

Lay must have an object. *Lay* tells what a person or thing does for someone or something else. The principal parts of *lay* are:

lay (simple form)	You should *lay* the *tiles* very evenly.
laid (past form)	Mary *laid* her *son* on his bed early this afternoon.
laid (past participle)	That hen has *laid* six *eggs* this week.
laying (present participle)	The workers are *laying* the *carpet* now.

6. **Rise/Raise**

Rise cannot take an object. *Rise* tells what someone or something does for himself or by itself. The principal parts of *rise* are:

rise (simple form)	The temperature *rises* sharply in the afternoon.
rose (past form)	The sun *rose* at seven yesterday.
risen (past participle)	Prices have *risen* a great deal lately.
rising (present participle)	The baby's temperature is *rising* by the hour.

Raise must have an object. *Raise* tells what someone or something does for someone or something else. The principal parts of *raise* are:

raise (simple form)	Please *raise* the *window* a little.
raised (past form)	The Browns *raised* their *children*.
raised (past participle)	The store has *raised* its *prices*.
raising (present participle)	The new book is *raising* many interesting *questions*.

7. **Learn/Teach**

Learn is a verb that can be followed *directly* by an infinitive as an object.

INFIN.
She *learned to speak* French.

Teach is a verb that can be followed by an infinitive as an object. However, this infinitive must have its own subject. (See *Pronouns-Personal-Case*, page 80.)

S   INFIN.
I *taught John to speak* French.

S   INFIN.
I *taught him to speak* French.

8. **Can/May**

Can is a modal that means *ability*.

Mary *can* speak French.

John *can* play the piano.

May is a modal that means *permission*.

May I leave now?

John *may* have the last piece of cake.

9. **Hanged/Hung**

Hanged and *hung* are both correct past participle forms of the verb *hang*. BUT:

Hanged refers to *executions* (*killings*) of persons.

PERSON
The *murderer* was *hanged* by the neck until dead.

Hung refers to things.

THING
The *picture* was *hung* over the fireplace.

Error Examples

WRONG: I believe we can handle this matter between the three of us.
RIGHT: I believe we can handle this matter *among* the three of us.

WRONG: The students had a large amount of problems.
RIGHT: The students had a large *number* of problems.

WRONG: The government has a large number of plutonium stored in a western state.
RIGHT: The government has a large *amount* of plutonium stored in a western state.

WRONG: The frightened man rushed in the police station.
RIGHT: The frightened man rushed *into* the police station.

WRONG: She sat her new chair between the sofa and the buffet.
RIGHT: She *set* her new chair between the sofa and the buffet.

WRONG: Miss Jones learned us to swim in a few days.
  RIGHT: Miss Jones *taught* us to swim in a few days.

WRONG: Can I please have your attention?
  RIGHT: *May* I please have your attention?

WRONG: The clothes were neatly hanged on the clothesline.
  RIGHT: The clothes were neatly *hung* on the clothesline.

WRONG: The live wire laid in the street for hours after the storm.
  RIGHT: The live wire *lay* in the street for hours after the storm.

WRONG: Susan likes to lay down for a short nap every afternoon.
  RIGHT: Susan likes to *lie* down for a short nap every afternoon.

WRONG: We certainly hope that prices do not raise so quickly again.
  RIGHT: We certainly hope that prices do not *rise* so quickly again.

Exercise

Directions: Write a "C" on the line if the sentence is correct. Write an "X" on the line if there is an error in usage.

_____ 1. The picture was hung over the fireplace.

_____ 2. That grandfather clock has sat in that same spot for forty years.

_____ 3. The volcano had lain dormant for fifty years when it suddenly erupted.

_____ 4. There was a surprising number of news coming from that country.

_____ 5. The bread dough has raised enough and is now ready to be baked.

_____ 6. The children's papers were hung about the classroom.

_____ 7. He distributed his wealth among his children, Betty, and John.

_____ 8. Ellen can run faster than Beth.

_____ 9. They have already risen their family and are now free to travel.

_____ 10. A large amount of people showed up for the grand opening.

_____ 11. The jeweler has carefully set the diamond into a new mounting.

_____ 12. The harried student dashed quickly in the classroom.

_____ 13. When Betty arrived home, she found her husband laying on the sofa asleep as usual.

_____ 14. Parents usually feel proud when their baby learns to take his first few steps.

_____ 15. Children often ask if they can have candy.

_____ 16. The car suddenly left the road, slammed into a low wall, and turned over several times.

_____ **17.** Never leave your purse lying where someone might be able to steal it.

_____ **18.** The army had hanged several deserters in the weeks before the war finally ended.

_____ **19.** John's father learned him to repair heavy equipment.

_____ **20.** Mrs. Jones had carefully lain her children's clothes out ready for the children to put on.

Check your answers using the error key on page 158.

Words Often Confused, Group I

The following words are often confused:

1. **Accept/Except**

>   _Accept_ is a verb that means "to give a positive answer" or "to receive."

>>   Susan _accepted_ his offer of a job. (gave a positive answer)

>>   The club _accepted_ three new members. (received)

>   _Except_ as a verb means "to exclude" or "to keep out."

>>   The boys _excepted_ John from their club. (They did not accept him.)

>   _Except_ is more commonly used as a preposition, meaning "with the exception of."

>>   PREP.
>>   Everybody _except_ Jane went to the party. (Jane was _not_ a member of the group that went to the party.)

2. **Advice/Advise**

>   _Advise_ is a _verb_.

>>   VERB
>>   The doctor _advised_ her to quit smoking.

>   _Advice_ is a noun.

>>   N
>>   He gave me some good _advice_.

3. **All Ready/Already**

>   _All ready_ is an _adjective phrase_ meaning "completely ready."

>>   ADJ. PHRASE
>>   We were _all ready_ to leave at eight o'clock.

>   _Already_ is an _adverb_ of time meaning "by or before a specific time."

>>   ADV.
>>   They had _already_ left at five o'clock. (by five o'clock)

>>   ADV.
>>   He had _already_ eaten when I arrived. (before I arrived)

4. **Altogether/All Together**

    Altogether is an *adverb* meaning "completely."

    ADV.
    I am *altogether* tired.

    All together is an *adjective phrase* meaning "in a group."

    ADJ. PHRASE
    The children are *all together* now and ready to go to the park.

5. **Beside/Besides**

    The preposition *besides* means "except."

    Everyone *besides* John went to the party.

    The preposition *beside* means "next to."

    John was standing *beside* me. (NOT: *besides* me)

6. **Cloth/Clothes**

    Cloth is a noun (usually used as a non-count noun) that means "material or fabric."

    NCN
    She bought some white *cloth* to make a wedding dress.

    Clothes is a plural count noun meaning "garments used to cover the body."

    PL. CN
    She bought a lot of *clothes* when she was in Paris.

    PL. CN
    Beautiful *clothes* are usually expensive.

7. **Desert/Dessert**

    A *desert* is "a dry area of the world with little vegetation."

    A large percentage of the world's surface is a *desert* where very little grows.

    A *dessert* is "a sweet food usually eaten at the end of a meal."

    We had apple pie and ice cream for *dessert*.

8. **Differ From/Differ With**

    To *differ from* is "to be dissimilar."

    Men *differ* physically *from* women.

    To *differ with* is "to disagree with."

    I *differ with* you on this issue. (I disagree with you.)

9. **Emigrate/Immigrate**

    To *emigrate* means "to leave one country to live in another."

    In the early part of this century many people *emigrated* from Europe. They went to live in the United States.

    To *immigrate* means "to move *to* a new country."

    In the early part of this century many people from Europe *immigrated* to the United States.

10. **Farther/Further**

> *Farther* means "to or at a more distant point in space." (actual distance)
>> We have to drive a few miles *farther*.
>
> *Further* means "to or at a more distant point in time, degree, or quantity." (figurative distance)
>> Let us consider this problem *further*. (time)
>>
>> We should do *further* research on this matter. (quantity)
>>
>> Be careful not to excite the children *further*. (degree)

Error Examples

WRONG: John did not except my invitation to the party.
 RIGHT: John did not *accept* my invitation to the party.

WRONG: You will find your umbrella besides the table.
 RIGHT: You will find your umbrella *beside* the table.

WRONG: Please advice him that he must hurry.
 RIGHT: Please *advise* him that he must hurry.

WRONG: Susan gave Paul some excellent advise.
 RIGHT: Susan gave Paul some excellent *advice*.

WRONG: Please ask the students not to stand altogether in the hall.
 RIGHT: Please ask the students not to stand *all together* in the hall.

WRONG: I am all together disgusted with his behavior.
 RIGHT: I am *altogether* disgusted with his behavior.

WRONG: Has John really finished his homework all ready?
 RIGHT: Has John really finished his homework *already*?

WRONG: Dinner is already to be served.
 RIGHT: Dinner is *all ready* to be served.

WRONG: Mary bought new cloth to wear to the party.
 RIGHT: Mary bought new *clothes* to wear to the party.

WRONG: Be careful to take lots of water when you cross the dessert.
 RIGHT: Be careful to take lots of water when you cross the *desert*.

WRONG: Would you like a piece of cake for desert?
 RIGHT: Would you like a piece of cake for *dessert*?

WRONG: New York differs with Washington, D.C.
 RIGHT: New York differs *from* Washington, D.C.

WRONG: When discussing politics, Bob frequently differs from his father.
RIGHT: When discussing politics, Bob frequently differs *with* his father.

WRONG: During times of economic hardship, people may have to immigrate from their native land.
RIGHT: During times of economic hardship, people may have to *emigrate* from their native land.

WRONG: I believe Martha's house is further down the road.
RIGHT: I believe Martha's house is *farther* down the road.

WRONG: Do you feel it is necessary to think about this matter farther?
RIGHT: Do you feel it is necessary to think about this matter *further*?

Exercise

Directions: Write a "C" on the line if the sentence is correct. Write an "X" on the line if there is an error in word choice.

_____   **1.** He has all ready spent next month's allowance.

_____   **2.** Mary looked all day for clothes suitable to cover the worn pillows.

_____   **3.** Will John take his doctor's advice?

_____   **4.** In a surprise vote the board excepted John from membership.

_____   **5.** Can you get everybody altogether for the meeting in ten minutes?

_____   **6.** Helen enjoys wearing the clothes she designs.

_____   **7.** The two political candidates certainly differed loudly from one another.

_____   **8.** One reason people will emigrate from their country is to escape political persecution.

_____   **9.** Did you look besides the sofa for your book?

_____   **10.** Do not try to drive further today.

_____   **11.** Will you accept my apologies?

_____   **12.** Why did so many people immigrate from Uruguay to go to Australia?

_____   **13.** I was surprised at the advise he gave me.

_____   **14.** Steve differs with his father in physical appearance.

_____   **15.** Let me give you some farther instruction.

Check your answers using the error key on page 158.

Words Often Confused, Group II

The following words are often confused:

1. **Formally/Formerly**

    Formally means "in a formal way."

    The meeting was conducted very *formally*.

    Formerly means "previously," or "at an earlier time."

    June was *formerly* a member of that club.

2. **Healthful/Healthy**

    Healthful means "good for one's health."

    Vegetables are *healthful* foods.

    Healthy means "in a good condition of health."

    All of his children are *healthy*.

3. **Illusion/Allusion**

    An *illusion* is "a false idea" or "unreal image."

    The magician created the *illusion* that he was flying through the air.

    An *allusion* is "an indirect reference."

    The professor made an *allusion* to Greek mythology.

4. **Imply/Infer**

    To imply is "to suggest without stating directly." Only the speaker or writer can *imply*.

    Susan *implied* that she was not happy with her job.

    To infer is "to make a conclusion based on evidence not directly stated." Only the listener or reader can *infer*.

    I *inferred* from her letter that Susan was not happy with her job.

5. **Its/It's**

    Its is the singular possessive pronoun for things.

    PRON.
    The tree lost *its* leaves when the weather turned cold.

    It's is the contraction for *it is*.

    It's a nice day today. (*It is* a nice day today.)

6. **Leave/Let**

    To leave means "to go away from."

    He *leaves* school at three o'clock every day.

    To let means "to permit."

    John *let* me borrow his car.

7. **Loose/Lose**

   The adjective *loose* means "not tight."

   ADJ.
   This blouse is too *loose*. I need a smaller size.

   To lose is a verb meaning "to leave behind by accident" or "to unintentionally cease having."

   VERB
   I often *lose* my car keys.

8. **Most/Almost**

   The adjective *most* is the superlative form of *many*, meaning "the largest number."

   ADJ.
   Most people like ice cream.

   The adjective *most* is also the superlative form of *much*, meaning "the largest amount."

   ADJ.
   Most coffee comes from Brazil.

   Almost is an adverb meaning "slightly less than," "not quite," or "very nearly."

   ADV.
   Almost all the students are here.

   ADV.
   He is *almost* ready to leave.

   ADV.
   He *almost* won the race.

9. **Plane/Plain**

   The noun *plane* often means "airplane."

   N
   His *plane* will arrive in Chicago at nine o'clock.

   The adjective *plain* means "simple," "not fancy," or "undecorated."

   ADJ.
   Her dress was very *plain*.

10. **Principal/Principle**

    The adjective *principal* means "chief" or "very important."

    The noun *principal* means "chief official."

    ADJ.
    The *principal* reason for his failure was his lack of interest in his job.

    N
    He wants to talk to the *principal* of the school.

    The noun *principle* means "fundamental truth."

    N
    He is studying the *principles* of accounting.

11. **Quiet/Quite**

    Quiet is an adjective meaning "not noisy."

                    ADJ.
        It was a very *quiet* party.

    Quite is an adverb meaning "completely" or "to a degree."

              ADV.
        He is *quite* nervous today.

              ADV.
        He is *quite* tall.

Error Examples

WRONG: He spoke formerly and eloquently on that serious subject.
 RIGHT: He spoke *formally* and eloquently on that serious subject.

WRONG: John was formally a member of that club, but he resigned.
 RIGHT: John was *formerly* a member of that club, but he resigned.

WRONG: Fruit is a very healthy food.
 RIGHT: Fruit is a very *healthful* food.

WRONG: The politician made a clever illusion to the political problems his chief rival was having.
 RIGHT: The politician made a clever *allusion* to the political problems his chief rival was having.

WRONG: Mary never said it directly, but she inferred that she did not like me.
 RIGHT: Mary never said it directly, but she *implied* that she did not like me.

WRONG: Would you please leave me do this job by myself.
 RIGHT: Would you please *let* me do this job by myself.

WRONG: Linda cannot wear this belt because it is too lose.
 RIGHT: Linda cannot wear this belt because it is too *loose*.

WRONG: Did you loose your watch?
 RIGHT: Did you *lose* your watch?

WRONG: Most everybody who is supposed to come is here already.
 RIGHT: *Almost* everybody who is supposed to come is here already.

WRONG: Which plain are you taking to New York?
 RIGHT: Which *plane* are you taking to New York?

WRONG: The principle of my daughter's school was educated in Europe.
 RIGHT: The *principal* of my daughter's school was educated in Europe.

WRONG: We spent a quite evening at home together.
 RIGHT: We spent a *quiet* evening at home together.

WRONG: The ship lost it's way from Florida to Bimini.
 RIGHT: The ship lost *its* way from Florida to Bimini.

Exercise

Directions: Write a "C" on the line if the sentence is correct. Write an "X" on the line if there is an error in word choice.

_____ **1.** Do you think that its difficult to learn a foreign language?

_____ **2.** The modern art piece they chose was plain but bold.

_____ **3.** The principle fact I would like you to remember concerns the human personality.

_____ **4.** Are you quite sure you wish to spend that much for one chair?

_____ **5.** His wife was formerly married to the Spanish Ambassador.

_____ **6.** Her parents are quite old, but relatively healthful.

_____ **7.** The young actress was able to create the allusion that she was middle-aged.

_____ **8.** From reading his letter, I inferred that he was having financial problems.

_____ **9.** He put his keys in his coat pocket so that he would not loose them.

_____ **10.** Can you let the student continue with this course if he makes up all missed work?

_____ **11.** Please leave him find out the truth by himself.

_____ **12.** I do not trust that man; he has absolutely no principles.

_____ **13.** I most fell off my seat laughing when I saw the clown chase the bull.

_____ **14.** I think my battery has a loose connection.

_____ **15.** Are you trying to infer that I should study more?

Check your answers using the error key on page 159.

Words Often Confused, Group III

The following words are often confused:

1. **Respectfully/Respectively**

   Respectfully means "with respect."

   > The audience rose *respectfully* when the president entered.

   Respectively means "in the order given."

   > The Thompsons lived in Chicago, Los Angeles, and New York *respectively*.

2. **So/So That**

   So is a conjunction joining a clause of *result* to a main clause.

   > It rained a lot that year, *so* there were lots of wildflowers to enjoy. (*result*)

   So that joins a clause of *purpose* to a main clause.

   > We wore raincoats *so that* we would not get our clothes wet. (*purpose*)

3. **Stationary/Stationery**

   Stationary means "in a fixed position."

   > The only time most children are *stationary* is when they are asleep.

   Stationery refers to writing supplies.

   > That *stationery* store sells fancy writing paper and envelopes.

4. **Their/There/They're**

   Their is the third-person plural possessive pronoun.

   > PRON.
   > They sold *their* home to a couple from London.

   There is (1) an adverb of place or (2) an expletive that tells of existence.

   > ADV.
   > Your package is *there* on the counter.

   > EXPLETIVE
   > *There* are fifty states in the United States.

   They're is the contraction of *they are*.

   > *They're* ready to see you now.

5. **To/Too/Two** (See also Chapter 3, "Modifiers," *Too*, *Very*, and *Enough*, page 41).

   To is (1) part of the infinitive form or (2) a preposition.

   > INFIN.
   > I like *to walk* in the rain.

   > PREP.
   > I walked *to* the store.

   Too is an adverb indicating an excess.

   > ADV.
   > It is *too* hot today to study.

   Two is a number (2).

   > I have *two* children, John and Greg.

6. **Weather/Whether**

> *Weather* is a noun meaning "atmospheric conditions."

>> N
>> It is nice *weather* today for a picnic.

> *Whether* is a conjunction meaning "if."

>> CONJ.
>> I do not know *whether* he will come to the party.

7. **Who's/Whose**

> *Who's* is the contraction for *who* is.

>> I do not know *who's* coming tonight.

> *Whose* is (1) a question word or (2) a possessive relative pronoun.

>> QW
>> *Whose* book is this?

>> PRON.
>> I met the man *whose* daughter is in my class.

Error Examples

WRONG: Last summer I visited the capital cities of Connecticut, Massachusetts, and Rhode Island respectfully.

RIGHT: Last summer I visited the capital cities of Connecticut, Massachusetts, and Rhode Island *respectively*.

WRONG: I bought a car so I would not have to walk to work.

RIGHT: I bought a car *so that* I would not have to walk to work.

WRONG: A model must sometimes remain stationery for hours at a time.

RIGHT: A model must sometimes remain *stationary* for hours at a time.

WRONG: Please put the piano over their near the window.

RIGHT: Please put the piano over *there* near the window.

WRONG: Robin is really much to nervous to be in public relations.

RIGHT: Robin is really much *too* nervous to be in public relations.

WRONG: Bob is not sure weather or not he will be able to attend your opening next week.

RIGHT: Bob is not sure *whether* or not he will be able to attend your opening next week.

WRONG: Who's purse do you think this is?

RIGHT: *Whose* purse do you think this is?

Exercise

Directions: Write a "C" on the line if the sentence is correct. Write an "X" on the line if there is an error in word choice.

_____ **1.** The whether is usually nice in Hawaii all year round.

_____ **2.** They're buying a home in the city next year.

_____ **3.** We met two of my father's business associates at the dinner.

_____ **4.** Did you find out whose coming early?

_____ **5.** I love to browse in stationary stores.

_____ **6.** Bob thinks this material is too difficult for first-year students.

_____ **7.** The students left there books on the floor during the exam.

_____ **8.** The audience applauded respectively at the end of her speech.

_____ **9.** Do not send any of these booklets too people who did not put their complete address on the form.

_____ **10.** He parked his car on the street so that he would not have to pay for parking in the garage.

Check your answers using the error key on page 159.

Correlative Conjunctions

The following is a list of _Correlative Conjunctions_. Remember that they are always used in the following pairs. Do not mix them up.

both . . . and

either . . . or

neither . . . nor

not only . . . but also

whether . . . or

> That music is _both_ disturbing _and_ loud.
>
> _Either_ he is going to get a job here _or_ he is going to study in Los Angeles.
>
> He is _neither_ well qualified _nor_ sufficiently experienced for that position.
>
> He refused to say _whether_ he would come to the meeting in person _or_ send a representative.
>
> That horse is _not only_ the youngest one in the race _but also_ the only one to win two years in a row.

Notes   a. Do not use _both_ . . . _and_ for three or more nouns or adjectives.

Mary, Blair, and Margie are going to arrive late.

OR

Mary and Blair, as well as Margie, are going to arrive late.

b. *Whether* may sometimes be used alone.

I do not know *whether* she received the package.

Error Examples

WRONG: Both John, Ernest, and Paul are going to the game.
RIGHT: John *and* Ernest, *as well as* Paul, are going to the game.

OR

John, *Ernest*, *and Paul* are going to the game.

WRONG: That book includes only not records but also cassettes.
RIGHT: That book includes *not only* records *but also* cassettes.

WRONG: She won the dance competition because she had both originality as well as grace.
RIGHT: She won the dance competition because she had *both* originality *and* grace.

WRONG: She decided not only to start a diet, but to join an exercise class also.
RIGHT: She decided *not only* to start a diet, *but also* to join an exercise class.

WRONG: That coin is not only valuable but rare also.
RIGHT: That coin is *not only* valuable *but also* rare.

WRONG: Neither the public or private sector of the economy will be seriously affected by this new regulation.
RIGHT: Neither the public *nor* private sector of the economy will be seriously affected by this new regulation.

WRONG: He refused to work either in Chicago nor in Detroit.
RIGHT: He refused to work *either* in Chicago *or* in Detroit.

Exercise

Directions: Write a "C" on the line if the sentence is correct. Write an "X" on the line if there is a correlative conjunction error.

_____ **1.** Some students can neither write or speak accurately.

_____ **2.** That course includes not only TOEFL preparation but also techniques of test taking.

_____ **3.** They like both living abroad as well as living at home.

_____ **4.** Tom won not only the 100-yard dash but the broad jump also.

_____ **5.** He is neither limber nor quick.

_____ **6.** Either you will attend class regularly or you can expect a low grade.

_____ **7.** Whether out of necessity or greed, he accepted the bribe.

_____ **8.** Both the president and the vice-president gave speeches last night.

_____ **9.** The play was both long, boring, and depressing.

_____ **10.** He is both deceptive as well as irresponsible.

Check your answers using the error key on page 159.

Subject/Verb Agreement

Singular subjects take singular verbs. Plural subjects take plural verbs.

       S   VERB
The *secretary* in this office *comes* to work at eight.

       S   VERB
The *secretaries* in this office *come* to work at eight.

Problems in determining the subject:

1. Subjects are never found in prepositional phrases.

     S   PREP. PHRASE VERB
The *price of all these items is* twenty dollars.

     S   PREP. PHRASE VERB
The *characters in this story are* well developed.

2. *Here* and *there* are not subjects. Look *after* the verb to find the subject.

   VERB   S
Here *comes* the *bus*.

   VERB   S
There *are* many good *reasons* to study language.

3. The subject also follows the verb in this pattern:

> <small>ADV.   VERB   S</small>
> *On the door was a wreath of flowers.*

> <small>ADV.   VERB   S</small>
> *Around the corner are* several small *shops*.

4. Expressions introduced with words such as *along with, besides, like, as well as*, and *including* do not change the number of the subject.

> <small>S.   VERB</small>
> *Mr. Jones*, along with his wife and six children, *is going* to Paris.

> <small>S   VERB</small>
> The *weather*, as well as economic conditions, *is* a consideration

> <small>S   VERB</small>
> Several *candidates*, including John Baker, *are going*.

5. When two subjects are joined by *either . . . or* or *neither . . . nor*, the subject closer to the verb determines its number.

> <small>S   S   VERB</small>
> Neither *Mary* nor her *sisters are going* to the party.

> <small>S   S   VERB</small>
> Either my *sisters* or my *mother is going* to the wedding.

6. Some words look plural but are singular. Among these words are *economics, mathematics, physics, news,* and *politics*.

> <small>S   VERB</small>
> The *news was* good.

> <small>S   VERB</small>
> *Mathematics is* a challenging field.

7. The subject of a relative clause, *who*, *which*, or *that*, is singular or plural depending on its *antecedent*.

> <small>ANTECEDENT S   VERB</small>
> The *students who come* to class every day generally *progress* rapidly.

> <small>ANTECEDENT S   VERB</small>
> Bob is one of my *friends who are helping* me paint my house.

> <small>ANTECEDENT   S   VERB</small>
> Bob is the only *one* of my friends *who is helping* me paint my house.

Error Examples

WRONG: His influence over the last ten years have grown considerably.
RIGHT: His influence over the last ten years *has* grown considerably.

WRONG: Over the fireplace hangs several small paintings.
RIGHT: Over the fireplace *hang* several small paintings.

WRONG: Neither the moon nor the stars is visible.
RIGHT: Neither the moon nor the stars *are* visible.

WRONG: A study of all possible causes of these multiple fractures are in order.
 RIGHT: A study of all possible causes of these multiple fractures *is* in order.

WRONG: There occurs to me a few possible explanations for his behavior.
 RIGHT: There *occur* to me a few possible explanations for his behavior.

WRONG: His furniture, including a dining room table and six chairs, are being sold.
 RIGHT: His furniture, including a dining room table and six chairs, *is* being sold.

WRONG: I asked all the students who was willing to help to meet me at the school.
 RIGHT: I asked all the students who *were* willing to help to meet me at the school.

WRONG: The college newspaper prints only the news that are of interest to the students and faculty.
 RIGHT: The college newspaper prints only the news that *is* of interest to the students and faculty.

WRONG: Either the students or the teacher were mistaken.
 RIGHT: Either the students or the teacher *was* mistaken.

Exercise

Directions: Write a "C" on the line if the sentence is correct. Write an "X" on the line if there is an error in subject-verb agreement.

_____ **1.** There are several jobs available.

_____ **2.** Along the beach was several small boats that had been washed ashore.

_____ **3.** Neither my sisters nor my brother is ready to begin college.

_____ **4.** The lack of logic in his arguments never cease to surprise me.

_____ **5.** She was determined to study nuclear physics, which was the most difficult course offered at that school.

_____ **6.** Students who have difficulty with this subject should try to find someone who is willing to tutor them.

_____ **7.** Either her husband or her children is going to be upset no matter what decision she makes.

_____ **8.** Betty is one of the women who is responsible for writing that.

_____ **9.** My uncle, as well as my father, are going to Canada on business.

_____ **10.** The only one of his friends who is upset with John is Bob.

Check your answers using the error key on page 159.

Parts Of Speech*

Sometimes a word can be identified as a noun, adjective, adverb, or verb by its suffix (ending).

1. The following suffixes usually indicate *nouns*:

-ion, -sion, -tion	popula*tion*
-acy	accur*acy*
-age	im*age*
-ance, -ence	perman*ence*
-hood	child*hood*
-ar, -or	schol*ar*, doct*or*
-ism	social*ism*
-ist	art*ist*
-ment	govern*ment*
-ness	happi*ness*
-y	beaut*y*
-ty	reali*ty*, capaci*ty*

2. The following suffixes usually indicate *adjectives*:

-al	natur*al*
-ful	beauti*ful*
-ly	friend*ly*
-ic	chron*ic*
-ish	child*ish*
-like	child*like*
-ous	popul*ous*, numer*ous*
-y	happ*y*
-ate	accur*ate*
-able, -ible	cap*able*, terr*ible*

3. The following suffix usually indicates *adverbs*:

-ly	happi*ly*, readi*ly*, beautiful*ly*

4. The following suffixes usually indicate *verbs*:

-ify	beaut*ify*
-ate	popul*ate*
-ize	real*ize*

Note   There are some exceptions to these general rules.

---

* See also Chapter 3, "Modifiers"—*Adjective/Adverb Confusion*, page 21.

Error Examples

WRONG: I was amazed at her natural beautiful.
  RIGHT: I was amazed at her natural *beauty*.

WRONG: His illness was chronically.
  RIGHT: His illness was *chronic*.

WRONG: Happily is a rare state of being.
  RIGHT: *Happiness* is a rare state of being.

WRONG: He had an unhappy childlike.
  RIGHT: He had an unhappy *childhood*.

WRONG: You should reality the truth.
  RIGHT: You should *realize* the truth.

WRONG: That country has a very large populate.
  RIGHT: That country has a very large *population*.

Exercise

Directions: Write a "C" on the line if the sentence is correct. Write an "X" on the line if there is an error in the part of speech according to the suffix.

_____ **1.** Bob hopes to beauty his home by painting and carpeting.

_____ **2.** Lawrence is a very happily man.

_____ **3.** Japan is a very populous nation.

_____ **4.** What do you think is the real of that situation?

_____ **5.** Her manner was friendly and natural.

_____ **6.** Dr. Smith's capacity for hard work was incredible.

_____ **7.** I never questioned his accurately.

_____ **8.** Jane was surprised that he spoke so childish.

_____ **9.** That new medicine will not be readily available until next year.

_____ **10.** Does the book list the populous of that country in 1950?

Check your answers using the error key on page 159.

Prepositions (General Use)

A preposition is generally used to show the relationship between its object and other words in the sentence. The kinds of relationships that can be shown are as follows:

1. **Place** (*in*, *on*, *under*, *over*, etc.)

     Your book is *in* the desk drawer.

2. **Direction** (*to*, *toward*, *into*, etc.)

     The student ran *into* the room.

3. **Time** (*in*, *on*, *at*, etc.)

     We can meet *at* three o'clock.

4. **Agent** (*by*)

     This book was written *by* an elderly woman.

5. **Instrument** (*by*, *with*)

     I heard the news *by* telephone. (*communication*)

     She came *by* plane. (*transportation*)

     He opened the door *with* a key. (*instrument*; *tool*)

   Note   Use *by* + N (no article) for *communication* and *transportation*.

                 Examples: *by phone, by radio, by telegram, by train, by car, by boat*

6. **Accompaniment** (*with*)

     They like spaghetti *with* red sauce.

     Mrs. Jones went to the bank *with* her husband.

7. **Purpose** (*for*) (See also Chapter 6, "Basic Patterns"—*To/For* (Purpose, page 111.))

     He went to the store *for* bread.

   Note   Never use *for* + V + *ing* to express the purpose of the verb.

                 Example: He went to the store for buying bread.
                                          WRONG

8. **Partition/Possession** (*of*)

     They painted the front *of* the building.

     He broke the top *of* the table.

9. **Measure** (*by*, *of*)

     We buy our rice *by* the pound.

     Please buy a quart *of* milk.

10. **Similarity** (*like*)

     John looks *like* his father.

11. **Capacity** (*as*)

     Bill worked *as* a lifeguard this summer.

Error Examples

WRONG: We damaged the front to the car.
 RIGHT: We damaged the front *of* the car.

WRONG: That store sells flour for the 25-pound sack.
 RIGHT: That store sells flour *by* the 25-pound sack.

WRONG: Betty worked like a secretary for a few months.
 RIGHT: Betty worked *as* a secretary for a few months.

WRONG: For dinner we had chicken by rice.
 RIGHT: For dinner we had chicken *with* rice.

WRONG: Your son is waiting for you to his office.
 RIGHT: Your son is waiting for you *in* his office.

WRONG: The next performance begins in sundown.
 RIGHT: The next performance begins *at* sundown.

WRONG: We went to the bank to money.
 RIGHT: We went to the bank *for* money.

WRONG: These artifacts are made with Indians living in Peru.
 RIGHT: These artifacts are made *by* Indians living in Peru.

WRONG: Jane went for Chicago with train.
 RIGHT: Jane went *to* Chicago *by* train.

WRONG: Susan sings as her mother.
 RIGHT: Susan sings *like* her mother.

Exercise

Directions: Write a "C" on the line if the sentence is correct. Write an "X" on the line if there is an error with the preposition.

_____ **1.** We drove the car into the driveway.

_____ **2.** They came to visit us with a car.

_____ **3.** The movie was reviewed by the critic.

_____ **4.** He came to the United States for an education.

_____ **5.** Did you notice that Bob walks as his father?

_____ **6.** He opened the door by key.

_____ **7.** Paula looks nothing like her sister.

_____ **8.** They purchased the fabric for the yard.

_____ **9.** Barbara enjoyed working as a bank teller for one summer.

_____ **10.** He went to the store for buying a newspaper.

_____ **11.** We would like to invite you to our home for dinner on your birthday.

_____ **12.** He did not notice that the leg for the chair was broken before he sat down.

_____ **13.** John went to the store to buy two pounds butter.

_____ **14.** Would you please bring us some coffee with our meal.

_____ **15.** They met at the movies 7:00.

Check your answers using the error key on page 159.

Prepositions in Combinations

1. The following *verb plus preposition* combinations always appear as follows and must be learned together:

agree on (something)	We *agree on* that point.
agree with (a person)	I *agree with* you on that matter.
approve of	Betty *approves of* exercising.
arrive at OR *in*	They *arrived in* Tokyo last night.
complain about	Please do not *complain about* the prices.
consent to	She *consented to* her daughter's marriage.
comment on	She *commented on* his new suit.
consist of	Water *consists of* hydrogen and oxygen.
depend on	I am *depending on* good weather for my party.
laugh at	We *laughed at* his silly behavior.
object to	Do you *object to* my smoking?
succeed in	He *succeeded in* making everyone angry.

Note   The correct verb form to use after a preposition is a *gerund* (*V* + *ing*). See Chapter 4, "Verbs"—*Verbals*, rule 3, page 64.

2. Some other *verb plus preposition* combinations take two objects.

compare . . . with OR *to*	Do not *compare* me *with* (OR *to*) my sister.
excuse . . . for	I cannot *excuse* you *for* being late.
prefer . . . to	She *prefers* coffee *to* tea.
remind . . . of	He *reminded* me *of* my appointment.
thank . . . for	I *thanked* him *for* letting me use his car.

3. There are many *adjective + preposition* combinations that occur with the verb *to be*.

be afraid of	Henry *is afraid of* dogs.
be accustomed to	I *was accustomed to* seeing him every day.
be aware of	Are you *aware of* his problem?
be bored with	Jane *is bored with* school.
be certain of	You cannot *be certain of* the date.
be disappointed with	Susan *was disappointed with* that restaurant.
be familiar with	Is Doctor Jones *familiar with* that new technique?
be famous for	Wisconsin *is famous for* its cheese.
be frightened by	Do not *be frightened by* the thunder and lightning.
be happy with	The Joneses *are very happy with* their new home.

be in favor of	*Are* you *in favor of* women's liberation?
be interested in	John *is interested in* attending a large university.
be opposed to	He *is* really *opposed to* buying a new car.
be satisfied with	He *is* not *satisfied with* his new radio.
be surprised at OR *by*	Do not *be surprised at* his behavior.
be tired of	Maria *is* very *tired of* working six days a week.
be worried about	Mark *is* very *worried about* his sick child.

4. Some prepositions exist in fixed phrases.

according to	*According to* the news, the government has fallen.
along with	Can you take this package, *along with* these letters, to the post office?
as well as	I enjoy art *as well as* history.
because of	*Because of* the rain, there will be no picnic.
by means of	The thief entered the house *by means of* an open window.
by way of	John went to Paris *by way of* London.
in addition to	*In addition to* going to school full-time, Patricia works part-time.
in case of	*In case of* fire, pull this alarm.
in consideration of	*In consideration of* all your help, I would like to take you to dinner.
in contrast to OR *with*	*In contrast to* last summer, this summer is cool.
in deference to	*In deference to* his age, we did not argue with him.
in hopes of	We came here *in hopes of* meeting the president.
in lieu of	He gave an oral report *in lieu of* a written report.
in pursuit of	The police were *in pursuit of* the thief.
in search of	They went into the mountains *in search of* gold.
in spite of	*In spite of* his good intentions, he did not study very much.
in the face of	*In the face of* a severe drought, the tribe moved to a new location.
in terms of	He was a good husband *in terms of* earning a good living.

Error Examples

WRONG: Is John familiar enough for this part of town to find your house?
 RIGHT: Is John familiar enough *with* this part of town to find your house?

WRONG: In spite the rain, the party has not been canceled.
 RIGHT: In spite *of* the rain, the party has not been canceled.

WRONG: My son was surprised with his teacher's decision.
 RIGHT: My son was surprised *at* (OR *by*) his teacher's decision.

WRONG: He continued to work in the face to his doctor's disapproval.
 RIGHT: He continued to work in the face *of* his doctor's disapproval.

WRONG: Clyde is bored for living in the country.
 RIGHT: Clyde is bored *with* living in the country.

WRONG: Bob is always complaining for the heat in Arizona in the summertime.
 RIGHT: Bob is always complaining *about* the heat in Arizona in the summertime.

WRONG: How do you think Rome compares by Paris?
 RIGHT: How do you think Rome compares *to* Paris?

WRONG: Veronica is tired by waiting for me to get ready.
 RIGHT: Veronica is tired *of* waiting for me to get ready.

WRONG: Do you object with my cutting some of your flowers?
 RIGHT: Do you object *to* my cutting some of your flowers?

WRONG: Do you think it is fair to excuse him by being late?
 RIGHT: Do you think it is fair to excuse him *for* being late?

WRONG: Betty reminds me to my sister.
 RIGHT: Betty reminds me *of* my sister.

WRONG: Who is in favor for adjourning the meeting early?
 RIGHT: Who is in favor *of* adjourning the meeting early?

WRONG: What time do you think you will arrive to London?
 RIGHT: What time do you think you will arrive *in* London?

WRONG: He asked if he could paint the apartment in lieu for a month's rent.
 RIGHT: He asked if he could paint the apartment in lieu *of* a month's rent.

WRONG: One cannot depend with luck to bring success.
 RIGHT: One cannot depend *on* luck to bring success.

WRONG: He studied art in addition with his regular course of studies.
 RIGHT: He studied art in addition *to* his regular course of studies.

WRONG: George is not accustomed at speaking in public.
 RIGHT: George is not accustomed *to* speaking in public.

WRONG: Clyde is quite satisfied by his new apartment.
 RIGHT: Clyde is quite satisfied *with* his new apartment.

WRONG: Can we agree with a date for our next meeting?
 RIGHT: Can we agree *on* a date for our next meeting?

Exercise

Directions: Put "C" if the sentence is correct. Put "X" if there is an error with the preposition.

_____   **1.** Did you agree to your father on which car you should buy?

_____   **2.** They arrived to Paris sometime early in the summer.

_____   **3.** Were the students accustomed to leaving early on Fridays?

_____   **4.** Whether we leave early or late depends about your schedule.

_____   **5.** The doctor objected to the patient's leaving the hospital a day early.

_____   **6.** David was surprised at the amount of time necessary to fix the car.

_____   **7.** Henry was not very satisfied with the lab report that he wrote.

_____   **8.** Switzerland is famous of its beautiful mountains.

_____   **9.** The soldier showed great courage in the face of death.

_____   **10.** This home certainly does not compare favorably at our old one.

_____   **11.** The committee was in favor of increasing his salary.

_____   **12.** Were you tired with waiting for her to call?

_____   **13.** He did not expect us to comment to his newly decorated office.

_____   **14.** Are you familiar to early American art?

_____   **15.** He spent his life in search for absolute truth.

Check your answers using the error key on page 160.

Chapter Quiz

Error Identification

Directions: For the Error Identification questions, each sentence contains four underlined words or phrases. Select the one word or phrase that must be changed in order for the sentence to be correct. Circle your answer in the book or mark your answer on a separate sheet of paper.

1. The design for the new community center combines both refreshing originality as well as an
   <u>for</u>   <u>combines</u>   <u>as well as</u>
   (A)   (B)   (C)
   impressive respect for the traditional architecture of the area.
   <u>for the traditional architecture</u>
   (D)

2. He described his best friend as <u>being</u> adventuresome, <u>witty</u>, <u>and</u> successful, but very
   (A)   (B)   (C)
   <u>plane-looking</u>.
   (D)

3. <u>In order to earn</u> enough money to complete his education, John worked last summer <u>like</u> a
   (A)   (B)
   lifeguard <u>at</u> a <u>girls'</u> camp.
   (C)   (D)

4. When I <u>was</u> at the grocery store, I <u>realized that</u> the prices of many items <u>had been rised</u>.
   (A)   (B)   (C)   (D)

5. The natives of that region gathered plants and hunted small animals, but
   <u>of</u>
   (A)
   supplies <u>were bought by them</u> in the market-place, which they visited <u>infrequently</u>.
   (B)   (C)   (D)

6. Our <u>trek</u> in the <u>Sahara Dessert</u> was <u>extremely</u> fascinating, totally challenging, and enormously
   (A)   (B)   (C)
   <u>relaxing</u>.
   (D)

7. The political polls indicated that <u>most</u> people were not as much in favor <u>with</u> the new law as
   (A)   (B)   (C)
   <u>was previously thought</u>.
   (D)

8. We did not hire him <u>because</u> his <u>only</u> experience was coaching a high school basketball team,
   (A)   (B)
   leading a <u>parochial</u> school choir, and <u>to work</u> as a substitute teacher.
   (C)   (D)

9. The new teacher was <u>both</u> surprised <u>and</u> delighted when she realized that her class consisted <u>with</u>
   (A)   (B)   (C)
   many students from <u>faraway</u> countries.
   (D)

10. According to my calculations, the cost of two dozen roses are fifty dollars, which is considerably
                                                                    (A)   (B)
    less than the sixty-two dollars I was charged.
              (C)   (D)

11. In contrast of his earlier behavior, the young man demonstrated surprising maturity in the face of
                (A)   (B)   (C)   (D)
    severe stress.

12. I told them to take there boots off outside so they would not bring in a lot of snow.
                      (A)   (B)   (C)   (D)

13. Try to image what life was like for the early settlers of that part of the world.
        (A)   (B) (C)   (D)

14. Emergency relief, including medicine, clothing, and foodstuffs, were sent to the earthquake zone
                      (A)   (B)   (C)
    immediately following news of the disaster.
               (D)

15. It was so ferociously hot yesterday that our supposed day of outdoor enjoyment ended with
                 (A)   (B)   (C)
    everyone's laying in the shade.
             (D)

Check your answers using the error key on page 160.

Sentence Completion

Directions: In the Sentence Completion questions, one or more words are left out of each
sentence. Under each sentence, you will see four words or phrases. Select the one word or phrase
that completes the sentence correctly, then write it in the space provided in the book or on a
separate sheet of paper.

1. The young couple liked to buy, redecorate,
   and _____ older homes for a profit.

   (A) resold
   (B) reselling
   (C) resell
   (D) to resell

2. The management was shocked to realize
   that its trusted employee was _____ of
   stealing a large sum of money from the
   company.

   (A) suspicioned
   (B) suspicioning
   (C) suspected
   (D) suspicion

3. Not only having graduated *magna cum laude* _____, Steve made his family very proud of him.

   (A) and also having finished first in the national competition
   (B) also having finished first in the national competition
   (C) but having finished first in the national competition
   (D) but also having finished first in the national competition

4. _____ his earlier study, Dr. Melon's new study indicates a general warming trend in global weather.

   (A) In contrast of
   (B) In contrast to
   (C) In contrast by
   (D) In contrast as

5. The workers have finished pouring the floors, and _____ waiting for the house to be framed.

   (A) there
   (B) they're
   (C) their
   (D) they

6. The reason he wants to take a leave of absence is _____.

   (A) because he is needing a complete rest
   (B) because he needs a complete rest
   (C) that he needs a complete rest
   (D) because a complete rest is needed by him

7. The teacher objected to the students' _____ their opened umbrellas near the door.

   (A) sitting
   (B) having sat
   (C) setting
   (D) sat

8. He was a dynamic figure who inspired awe, devotion, and _____ in his followers.

   (A) love
   (B) loving feelings
   (C) feelings of love
   (D) loveliness

9. The rich young newlyweds bought a beautiful new home and _____.

   (A) their pool was installed
   (B) had a pool installed
   (C) had a pool being installed
   (D) a pool was installed

10. My boss _____ my taking two weeks' leave without pay.

    (A) consented to
    (B) consented for
    (C) consented of
    (D) consented about

11. The students worked on the problem for several minutes before _____.

    (A) they came to the realization that this problem was one that had no solution
    (B) realizing that it was insolvable
    (C) they were able to understand that this problem which seemed merely difficult was, in reality, insolvable
    (D) the insolvability of the problem was realized by them

12. Henry went to the conference _____ about government contracts.

    (A) to learn
    (B) with the purpose of learning
    (C) in order to have the opportunity to learn
    (D) in order to be in a position to learn

13. Try as he might, he could never manage to get an _____ balance in his checkbook.

   (A) accuracy
   (B) accurately
   (C) accurate
   (D) accurateness

14. The professor asked the students _____.

   (A) not only to write a report or give a speech
   (B) either to write a report or give a speech
   (C) neither to write a report or give a speech
   (D) neither to write a report but give a speech

15. She writes such _____ poetry that it is hard to believe she has never had a formal education.

   (A) beauty
   (B) beautiful
   (C) beautifully
   (D) beautify

Check your answers using the error key on page 160.

ERROR KEYS

(All references to rules and notes refer to the specific section where the quiz appears.)

Voice

__A__ 1. (*I ate steak* last night.) See rule 3.

__C__ 2.

__C__ 3.

__C__ 4.

__A__ 5. (*The road was built* in two years at a cost of five million dollars.) See rule 1.

__A__ 6. (The people loved their leader and *forgave his mistakes*.) See rule 4.

__A__ 7. (*John answered the phone* on the first ring.) See rule 3.

__C__ 8.

__C__ 9.

__C__ 10.

__C__ 11.

__A__ 12. (As we neared the house, *we could see a small dog* sitting on the porch.) See rule 4.

__A__ 13. (*A lot of crimes were committed* in this neighborhood last month.) See rule 1.

__A__ 14. (If you studied more, *you could easily pass your tests*.) See rules 1 and 4.

__C__ 15.

__C__ 16.

__A__ 17. (*I turned on the light* as I entered my bedroom.) See rules 1 and 4.

__A__ 18. (That electronics company is expanding and *developing many new products*.) See rule 4.

__A__ 19. (*The Battle of Hastings was fought* in 1066.) See rule 2.

__A__ 20. (*Jane put on her earrings* before she went to the party.) See rule 3.

__C__ 21.

__A__ 22. (Claire painted the living room and *laid a new carpet*.) See rule 4.

__A__ 23. (Jack works hard during the week and *spends his free time sailing his new boat*.) See rule 4.

__A__ 24. (*The carefully selected students represented the class well*.) See rule 4.

__A__ 25. (Bob *plays the piano and the guitar*.) See rule 5.

Parallelism

__X__ 1. (and *to swim*). See rule 1d.

__C__ 2.

__C__ 3.

__X__ 4. (*and the fjords*). See rule 2a.

__C__ 5.

__X__ 6. (*written* a will). See rule 1f.

__C__ 7.

__C__ 8.

__X__ 9. (and *confidence*). See rule 1a.

__C__ 10.

__X__ 11. (or *to study*). See rule 2d.

__X__ 12. (slow *to praise*). See rule 2f.

__C__ 13.

__X__ 14. (and *put* them). See rule 1e.

__X__ 15. (than *playing* golf). See rule 2e.

Wordiness

__W__ 1. (*The man shook his head*.) OR (*The man said no*.) See rule 3.

__C__ 2.

__C__ 3.

__W__ 4. (Jane went to the store *to buy a new dress*.) See rule 3.

__W__ 5. (*Running through the street*, the thief was apprehended by the police.) See rule 3.

__C__ 6.

__W__ 7. (Bob saw several *expensive* pieces of art.) See rule 2.

__C__ 8.

W	9.	(The ballerina *danced for hours*.) See rule 4.
W	10.	(Professor Blanton, *the college president*, will speak on this topic.) See rule 2.
C	11.	
C	12.	
W	13.	(*It took us three hours to drive to New York*.) See rule 3.
C	14.	
W	15.	(*I read the book* in four hours.) See rule 1.

Substandard

C	1.	
X	2.	(the reason he was late was *that*). See rule 8.
C	3.	
X	4.	(*a kind of* car). See rule 4.
X	5.	(*"Parallel" means that* objects are). See rule 9.
C	6.	
X	7.	(*nowhere*). See rule 2.
C	8.	
X	9.	(*all right*). See rule 3.
C	10.	
X	11.	(*are not* coming). See rule 1.
X	12.	(you do not *suspect*). See rule 7.
X	13.	(A "knock-out" is "a blow that causes unconsciousness.") See rule 9.
C	14.	
X	15.	(*anywhere*). See rule 2.
X	16.	(different *from*). See rule 10.
X	17.	(*off the* table). See rule 6.
C	18.	
X	19.	(very *angry with* his professor). See rule 5.
X	20.	(*kind of person*). See rule 4.

Usage

C	1.	
C	2.	
C	3.	
X	4.	(surprising *amount* of news). See rule 2.
X	5.	(has *risen* enough). See rule 6.
C	6.	
X	7.	(*between* his children, Betty and John). See rule 1.
C	8.	
X	9.	(have already *raised*). See rule 6.
X	10.	(large *number*). See rule 2.
C	11.	
X	12.	(dashed quickly *into*). See rule 3.
X	13.	(*lying* on the sofa). See rule 5.
C	14.	
X	15.	(if they *may* have candy). See rule 8.
C	16.	
C	17.	
C	18.	
X	19.	(*taught* him to repair). See rule 7.
X	20.	(had carefully *laid*). See rule 5.

Words Often Confused, Group I

X	1.	(*already*). See rule 5.
X	2.	(*cloth*). See rule 6.
C	3.	
C	4.	
X	5.	(*all together*). See rule 4.
C	6.	
X	7.	(differed loudly *with*). See rule 8.
C	8.	
X	9.	(*beside* the sofa). See rule 2.
X	10.	(*farther*). See rule 10.
C	11.	
X	12.	(*emigrate* from). See rule 9.
X	13.	(*advice*). See rule 3.
X	14.	(*differs from*). See rule 8.
X	15.	(*further* instruction). See rule 10.

Words Often Confused, Group II

X	1.	(*it's* difficult). See rule 5.
C	2.	
X	3.	(*principal* fact) OR (The *principle* I would like). See rule 10.
C	4.	
C	5.	
X	6.	(relatively *healthy*). See rule 2.
X	7.	(create the *illusion*). See rule 3.
C	8.	
X	9.	(would not *lose* them). See rule 7.
C	10.	
X	11.	(*let* him find out). See rule 6.
C	12.	
X	13.	(*almost* fell off my seat laughing). See rule 8.
C	14.	
X	15.	(trying to *imply*). See rule 4.

Words Often Confused, Group III

X	1.	(The *weather* is). See rule 6.
C	2.	
C	3.	
X	4.	(*who's* coming). See rule 7.
X	5.	(*stationery* stores). See rule 3.
C	6.	
X	7.	(*their* books). See rule 4.
X	8.	(applauded *respectfully*). See rule 1.
X	9.	(*to* people). See rule 5.
C	10.	

Correlative Conjunctions

X	1.	(neither write *nor* speak)
C	2.	
X	3.	(both living abroad *and* living).
X	4.	(not only the 100-yard dash, *but also* the broad jump)
C	5.	
C	6.	
C	7.	

C	8.	
X	9.	(*was long*, boring, *and* depressing) OR (long *and* boring, *as well as* depressing). See note a.
X	10.	(both deceptive *and* irresponsible)

Subject/Verb Agreement

C	1.	
X	2.	(*were* several small boats). See rule 3.
C	3.	
X	4.	(never *ceases*). See rule 1.
C	5.	
C	6.	
X	7.	(or her children *are* going). See rule 5.
X	8.	(the women who *are* responsible). See rule 7.
X	9.	(*is* going). See rule 4.
C	10.	

Parts of Speech

X	1.	(Bob hopes to *beautify*). See rule 4.
X	2.	(a very *happy* man). See rule 2.
C	3.	
X	4.	(the *reality* of that situation). See rule 1.
C	5.	
C	6.	
X	7.	(his *accuracy*). See rule 1.
X	8.	(so *childishly*). See rule 3.
C	9.	
X	10.	(the *population*). See rule 1.

Prepositions (General Use)

C	1.	
X	2.	(*by* car). See rule 5.
C	3.	
C	4.	
X	5.	(walks *like* his father). See rule 10.
X	6.	(*with a* key). See rule 5.
C	7.	

X   **8.** (*by* the yard) See rule 9.

C   **9.**

X   **10.** (*for* a newspaper). See rule 7.

C   **11.**

X   **12.** (leg *of* the chair). See rule 8.

X   **13.** (pounds *of* butter). See rule 9.

C   **14.**

X   **15.** (*at* 7:00). See rule 3.

Prepositions in Combinations

X   **1.** (agree *with* your father). See rule 1.

X   **2.** (arrived *in*). See rule 1.

C   **3.**

X   **4.** (depends *on* your schedule). See rule 1.

C   **5.**

X   **6.** (surprised *at*) OR (surprised *by*). See rule 3.

C   **7.**

X   **8.** (famous *for* its beautiful mountains). See rule 3.

C   **9.**

X   **10.** (compare favorably *to*) OR (compare favorably *with*). See rule 2.

C   **11.**

X   **12.** (tired *of* waiting). See rule 3.

X   **13.** (comment *on*). See rule 1.

X   **14.** (familiar *with*). See rule 3.

X   **15.** (in search *of*). See rule 4.

Chapter Quiz

Some of the incorrect answers contain more than one kind of error. However, in general, we have limited our error-references to those points contained in *Style*.

Error Identification

(C)   **1.** (*and*). See *Correlative Conjunctions*, page 159.

(D)   **2.** (*plain*-looking). See *Words Often Confused*, Group II, page 159.

(B)   **3.** (*as*). See *Prepositions (General Use)*, page 159.

(D)   **4.** (had been *raised*). See *Usage*, page 158.

(B)   **5.** (*bought supplies*). See *Voice*, page 157.

(B)   **6.** (*Sahara Desert*). See *Words Often Confused*, Group I, page 158.

(C)   **7.** (in favor *of*). See *Prepositions in Combinations*, page 160.

(D)   **8.** (*working*). See *Parallelism*, page 157.

(C)   **9.** (consisted *of*). See *Prepositions in Combinations*, page 160.

(A)   **10.** (*is*). See *Subject/Verb Agreement*, page 159.

(A)   **11.** (contrast *to*). See *Prepositions in Combinations*, page 160

(A)   **12.** (*their*). See *Words Often Confused*, Group III, page 159.

(A)   **13.** (to *imagine*). See *Parts of Speech*, page 159.

(C)   **14.** (*was sent*). See *Subject/Verb Agreement*, page 159.

(D)   **15.** (*lying*). See *Usage*, page 158.

Sentence Completion

(C)   **1.** (A) See *Parallelism*, page 157.
         (B) See *Parallelism*, page 157.
         (C) **Correct**
         (D) See *Parallelism*, page 157.

(C)   **2.** (A) See *Substandard*, page 158.
         (B) See *Substandard*, page 158.
         (C) **Correct**
         (D) See *Substandard*, page 158.

(D)   **3.** (A) See *Correlative Conjunctions*, page 159.
         (B) See *Correlative Conjunctions*, page 159.
         (C) See *Correlative Conjunctions*, page 159.
         (D) **Correct**

___(B)___ **4.** (A) See *Prepositions in Combinations*, page 160.
Correct
    (B) **Correct**
    (C) See *Prepositions in Combinations*, page 160.
    (D) See *Prepositions in Combinations*, page 160.

___(B)___ **5.** (A) See *Words Often Confused*, Group III, page 159.
    (B) **Correct**
    (C) See *Words Often Confused*, Group III, page 159.
    (D) See *Words Often Confused*, Group III, page 159.

___(C)___ **6.** (A) See *Substandard*, page 158.
    (B) See *Substandard*, page 158.
    (C) **Correct**
    (D) See *Substandard*, page 158 and *Voice*, page 158.

___(C)___ **7.** (A) See *Usage*, page 158.
    (B) See *Usage*, page 158.
    (C) **Correct**
    (D) See *Usage*, page 158.

___(A)___ **8.** (A) **Correct**
    (B) See *Parallelism*, page 157.
    (C) See *Parallelism*, page 157.
    (D) The meaning of *loveliness* does not fit here.

___(B)___ **9.** (A) See *Voice*, page 157.
    (B) **Correct**
    (C) See Chapter 4, "Verbs"—*Verbals*, page 64.
    (D) See *Voice*, page 157.

___(A)___ **10.** (A) **Correct**
    (B) See *Prepositions in Combinations*, page 160.
    (C) See *Prepositions in Combinations*, page 160.
    (D) See *Prepositions in Combinations*, page 160.

___(B)___ **11.** (A) See *Wordiness*, page 157.
    (B) **Correct**
    (C) See *Wordiness*, page 157.
    (D) See *Voice*, page 157.

___(C)___ **12.** (A) **Correct**
    (B) See *Wordiness*, page 157.
    (C) See *Wordiness*, page 157.
    (D) See *Wordiness*, page 157.

___(C)___ **13.** (A) See *Parts of Speech*, page 159.
    (B) See *Parts of Speech*, page 159.
    (C) **Correct**
    (D) See *Parts of Speech*, page 159.

___(B)___ **14.** (A) See *Correlative Conjunctions*, page 159.
    (B) **Correct**
    (C) See *Correlative Conjunctions*, page 159.
    (D) See *Correlative Conjunctions*, page 159.

___(B)___ **15.** (A) See *Parts of Speech*, page 159.
    (B) **Correct**
    (C) See *Parts of Speech*, page 159.
    (D) See *Parts of Speech*, page 159.

Practice Tests

Introduction To Practice Tests

The following three tests simulate the types of questions you will encounter in the Structure section of the TOEFL test. The types of questions are not interspersed, as in the actual TOEFL CBT, but they offer the kind of practice you need and will help you become familiar with the question formats for the TOEFL test. Each test is designed to be completed in 25 minutes (37 to 38 seconds per question). Make sure to set a timer or ask a friend to time you. After completing these tests, check your answers using the error keys that follow the exams, which will refer you to the specific grammatical points you'll need to review. Mark your answers in the space provided in the book, as you did with the Exercises in the chapters, or you can record your answers on a separate sheet of scrap paper, so that you can retake the tests if necessary.

PRACTICE TEST 1

Time Allowed—25 Minutes

Error Identification

> **Directions:** For the Error Identification questions, each sentence contains four underlined words or phrases. Select the one word or phrase that must be changed in order for the sentence to be correct. Circle your answer in the book or mark your answer on a separate sheet of paper.

1. Since William had been seriously ill for several months, his parents were concerned about
   (A)   (B)   (C)
   him wanting to return to school full-time.
   (D)

2. The mother cried as her child laid on the examination table after the accident.
                      (A)   (B) (C)   (D)

3. The students were quite surprised to find these kind of archeological ruins in the particular area
                                          (A)   (B)
   that they had chosen for the dig.
   (C) (D)

4. John stayed up all night long trying to solve a physic problem.
                     (A)   (B) (C)   (D)

5. Michael wants to become a general practitioner as his father and to move to a small town
                   (A)   (B)
   as soon as he graduates.
      (C)   (D)

6. In spite of their trepidation, the parents let their two oldest children driven alone to New Mexico
                       (A)   (B)   (C)
   to ski.
   (D)

7. Life in modern society lacks the sense of permanent that is so important to social stability.
                           (A)   (B)   (C)   (D)

8. As soon as they will finish the new business administration building, our offices are going to be
              (A)   (B)   (C)   (D)
   moved.

9. In spite of suffering some minor inconveniences, Dr. Blake and his wife enjoyed living in a
              (A)   (B)   (C)
   three-hundred-years-old house in London last summer.
         (D)

10. If Tom would have sent in his papers sooner, he would have been accepted for this semester.
               (A)   (B)   (C)   (D)

11. Professor Layton was <u>equally</u> fond of his two children, but he had to admit that he found the
                    <u>(A)</u>   <u>(B)</u>
    <u>youngest</u> an easier child <u>to handle</u>.
      (C)   (D)

12. <u>By</u> the beginning of next year, <u>much</u> of the people <u>who</u> live in that area may have difficulty
    <u>(A)</u>   (B)   (C)
    <u>finding</u> employment.
      (D)

13. <u>Even though</u> the child pretended <u>sleeping</u>, <u>when</u> we opened the bedroom door we were not
        (A)   (B)   (C)
    <u>deceived</u>.
      (D)

14. Be careful <u>to give</u> the caterers a <u>accurate</u> count of the number of people <u>whom</u> you expect <u>to go</u>
             <u>(A)</u>   (B)   (C)   (D)
    to the wedding reception.

15. Ever <u>since</u> he arrived, he <u>has been</u> complaining <u>about</u> <u>constantly</u> the weather.
        (A)   (B)   (C) (D)

16. The <u>living</u> room was <u>enough large</u> to accommodate <u>two long sofas</u> <u>easily</u>.
        (A)   (B)   (C)   (D)

17. <u>Approving</u> of my choice of colleges, my father said that he was <u>willing</u> <u>to completely pay</u> for all
    <u>(A)</u>   (B)   (C)
    the costs of my education.
          (D)

18. <u>In spite of</u> the <u>exceedingly</u> favorable financial benefits she is receiving, Linda now wishes that she
      (A)   (B)
    <u>was not stationed</u> in Alaska <u>for three years</u>.
         (C)   (D)

19. When the <u>seamstress</u> tried to sew the button on <u>with</u> <u>a</u> plastic needle, <u>it</u> broke.
            (A)   (B) (C)   (D)

20. We all <u>laughed</u> <u>when</u> Helen said she <u>could not</u> remember what day <u>was it</u>.
           (A)   (B)   (C)   (D)

21. The children soon forgot that it was <u>them</u>, <u>their</u> parents, <u>who</u> had encouraged them <u>to continue</u>
                                  (A)   (B)   (C)   (D)
    their education.

22. <u>Having ran</u> for three miles, I was exhausted <u>but</u> <u>exhilarated</u>.
      (A)   (B)   (C)   (D)

23. Harold announced <u>that</u> he could <u>not longer</u> tolerate the conditions of the contract <u>under which</u> he
                      (A)   (B)   (C)   (D)
    was working.

GO ON TO THE NEXT PAGE

24. Our company looks forward to <u>have</u> you on <u>staff</u>, and we <u>will</u> assist you in any way <u>possible</u> in
           (A)   (B)   (C)   (D)

    order to make your move pleasant.

25. The theater arranged a private <u>showing</u> of the film for Peter and <u>I</u> <u>so that</u> we could review it <u>before</u>
                                   (A)   (B) (C)   (D)

    our deadline.

Sentence Completion

Directions: In the Sentence Completion questions, one or more words are left out of each sentence. Under each sentence, you will see four words or phrases. Select the one word or phrase that completes the sentence correctly, then write it in the space provided in the book or on a separate sheet of paper.

26. It was _____ that we went for a hike in the mountains.

    (A) so nice a day
    (B) such nice day
    (C) so nice day
    (D) such nice a day

27. I was surprised to see _____ at the concert.

    (A) those number of people
    (B) that amount of people
    (C) that number of people
    (D) those amount of people

28. The art museum is internationally acclaimed not only for its sixteenth-century Flemish collection _____ for its early Picasso collection.

    (A) and
    (B) but
    (C) but also
    (D) as well as

29. _____ that the hope for cancer control may lie in the use of a vaccine.

    (A) To believe
    (B) It is believed
    (C) Believing
    (D) The belief

30. Everyone was _____ the threat of military intervention in that area.

    (A) frightened for
    (B) frightened
    (C) frightened to
    (D) frightened by

31. If Dorothy had not been badly hurt in a car accident, _____ in last month's marathon.

    (A) she would participate
    (B) she participated
    (C) she would have participated
    (D) she would had participate

32. On our last trip to Europe, we spent a lot of time visiting _____ churches and castles.

    (A) old enough
    (B) very old
    (C) enough old
    (D) too old

33. Our success depends _____ the project by December.

    (A) on finishing
    (B) finishing
    (C) about finishing
    (D) on to finish

34. Be sure to wake _____ at 7:00 A.M.

    (A) we
    (B) Paul and me
    (C) us, Paul and I
    (D) Paul and I

35. When Betty met Sue, _____.

    (A) she was a student at Stanford
    (B) Sue was a student at Stanford
    (C) she is a student at Stanford
    (D) at Stanford Sue was a student

36. Nancy sometimes wishes that she _____ in a small town.

    (A) was not living
    (B) did not lived
    (C) does not live
    (D) were not living

37. When the professor called on him, _____.

    (A) John repeated again the correct answer
    (B) John repeated the correct answer
    (C) John repeated the answer which was correct
    (D) the correct answer was repeated by John

38. These seats are reserved for _____.

    (A) those on the executive committee
    (B) they on the executive committee
    (C) them on the executive committee
    (D) those who find themselves in the position of being on the executive committee

39. Barbara has been pursuing a career in architecture _____ she graduated in May.

    (A) when
    (B) until
    (C) for
    (D) since

40. Our buyer has gone to New York _____ new fall clothes.

    (A) to choose
    (B) for to choose
    (C) for choosing
    (D) for having chosen

Check your answers using the error key on page 176.

GO ON TO THE NEXT PAGE

PRACTICE TEST 2

Time Allowed—25 Minutes

Error Identification

> **Directions:** For the Error Identification questions, each sentence contains four underlined words or phrases. Select the one word or phrase that must be changed in order for the sentence to be correct. Circle your answer in the book or mark your answer on a separate sheet of paper.

1. Lawrence never lost the respect for his parents who had struggled so hard to put him through
                (A)   (B)   (C)   (D)
   medical school.

2. I doubt weather he will enter the doctoral program this fall because of his financial problems.
          (A)   (B)   (C)   (D)

3. If Jackie and Mary had been in better physical condition, they might enjoyed the hike more.
                    (A)   (B) (C)   (D)

4. Not having passed the law exam, the state refused to issue him a license to practice.
         (A)   (B)   (C)   (D)

5. The interesting designed stairway led directly to a large ballroom where everyone was waiting for us.
        (A)   (B)   (C)   (D)

6. Even though they have been looking for an apartment for a month now, they have not been able
      (A)   (B)   (C)
   to find one anywheres.
         (D)

7. I have reserved six front-row seats for the basketball play-off game last night.
     (A)   (B)   (C)   (D)

8. The five hours of classes the students have every day are audio-lingual, reading, writing,
                                       (A)
   laboratory, and to choose an extra special-interest course.
    (B)   (C)   (D)

9. The crops are already showing signs of dehydration and probably cannot survive another week
               (A)   (B)   (C)
   without no rain.
      (D)

10. The children had such difficult time when they began school in their new neighborhood that their
           (A)   (B)
    parents decided never to move again.
          (C)   (D)

11. He had his tailor made an exotic oriental-looking robe for opening night.
     (A)   (B)   (C)   (D)

12. Teamwork requires that a player pass the ball to whomever is in the best position to make the
              (A)   (B)   (C)   (D)
    goal.

13. There were never any secrets among my sister and me when we were growing up.
                                     (A)   (B) (C)   (D)

14. Dr. Lacey was the kind of administrator which tried to maintain high morale among his staff by
                                              (A)   (B)   (C)
    encouraging open communication.
        (D)

15. Let's take one of this pamphlets and look up the special flights to Hawaii in November.
                          (A)   (B)   (C)   (D)

16. Samuel's new position as head of the editorial staff is certainly a more demanding one than
                          (A)   (B)   (C)
    Henry.
     (D)

17. Susan was determined to leave the office by 4:30 for catching the early train home.
                          (A)   (B)   (C)   (D)

18. The newlyweds found a style of living in Italy as satisfying that they wished that they could stay
                                            (A) (B)   (C)   (D)
    there forever.

19. Those who had already purchased tickets were instructed to go to gate first immediately.
    (A)   (B)   (C)   (D)

20. The cost of gasoline has raised tremendously in the last eight-month period.
                      (A)   (B)   (C)   (D)

21. It is important that you turned off the heater every morning before you leave for class.
    (A)   (B)   (C)   (D)

22. With regard to your letter of October 26, we are quiet disappointed to learn that you are unable to
                    (A)   (B)   (C)   (D)
    accept the job at this time.

23. Dr. Alvarez looked tiredly as he approached the podium to give his farewell speech to the
                       (A) (B)   (C)
    graduating class.
        (D)

24. Their office has not still returned the original document to us.
    (A)   (B) (C)   (D)

25. I was very embarrassed at the inauguration last week when I set in the wrong chair on the stage.
          (A)   (B)   (C)   (D)

GO ON TO THE NEXT PAGE

Sentence Completion

Directions: In the Sentence Completion questions, one or more words are left out of each sentence. Under each sentence, you will see four words or phrases. Select the one word or phrase that completes the sentence correctly, then write it in the space provided in the book or on a separate sheet of paper.

26. There _____ in that part of the country.

   (A) are not much industry
   (B) is not many industry
   (C) are not many industry
   (D) is not much industry

27. The *Marcus Aurelius*, _____ went down at sea in 1970, is reputed to have had great wealth on board.

   (A) that which
   (B) which
   (C) who
   (D) what

28. _____ since he lost his job.

   (A) He has been feeling bad
   (B) He is feeling badly
   (C) He had been feeling badly
   (D) He is feeling bad

29. Let's put a new _____ on the window sill.

   (A) flower's box
   (B) flowers' box
   (C) flower box
   (D) flowers box

30. I let my cousin _____ my car when he came to visit me.

   (A) to borrow
   (B) borrow
   (C) borrowing
   (D) borrowed

31. John remembered his parents' anniversary and _____.

   (A) sent them some flowers
   (B) to them sent some flowers
   (C) sent to them some flowers
   (D) some flowers to them sent

32. The plans for that building were drawn up in 1965 but _____.

   (A) their implementation was not put into action until 1970
   (B) the plans for that building were not implemented until 1970
   (C) were not implemented and started until 1970
   (D) were not implemented until 1970

33. The doctor _____.

   (A) adviced that Jim lie down every afternoon
   (B) adviced that Jim lay down every afternoon
   (C) advised that Jim lie down every afternoon
   (D) advised that Jim lay down every afternoon

34. John will most likely _____, but Kathy will probably stay home.

   (A) coming
   (B) be come
   (C) come
   (D) had come

35. _____ told us to turn our topics in by Friday.

    (A) Our professor he
    (B) Our professor who
    (C) Our professor
    (D) Our professor that

36. During her vacation in Europe, Margaret visited museums, went shopping, and _____ a lot of interesting people.

    (A) had met
    (B) was meeting
    (C) met
    (D) has been meeting

37. It was essential that we _____ the lease before the end of the month.

    (A) sign
    (B) signed
    (C) had signed
    (D) were signing

38. The opening of the new freeway has made traffic conditions in the city _____.

    (A) more good
    (B) the better
    (C) better
    (D) more better

39. If their train arrives _____ not make it to the theater on time.

    (A) lately, we will
    (B) late, we would
    (C) more later, we will
    (D) late, we will

40. When traveling in a foreign country, one should be careful to carry _____ at all times.

    (A) their passport
    (B) your passport
    (C) one's passport
    (D) hers passport

Check your answers using the error key on page 178.

GO ON TO THE NEXT PAGE

PRACTICE TEST 3

Time Allowed—25 Minutes

Error Identification

Directions: For the Error Identification questions, each sentence contains four underlined words or phrases. Select the one word or phrase that must be changed in order for the sentence to be correct. Circle your answer in the book or mark your answer on a separate sheet of paper.

1. One should always avoid to change lanes without first signaling.
    (A)   (B)   (C)   (D)

2. Their custom it is to name the first child after the paternal grandfather.
        (A)   (B)   (C)   (D)

3. While staying in Los Angeles, we were able not only to conduct our business but as well as to
        (A)   (B)   (C)
    visit many popular tourist attractions.
        (D)

4. Kathy studies very hard, and she is seen in the library night and day.
                    (A)   (B) (C)   (D)

5. Physics is a demanding field that has attracted many people to challenge their complexities.
                    (A)   (B)   (C)   (D)

6. The president gave to his advisers the new five-month austerity plan.
            (A)   (B)   (C)   (D)

7. The board of directors felt that Clark Weston was more better suited for the position than William Orly.
                        (A)   (B)   (C)   (D)

8. Having lost his job, Edward was only able to finish one semester of college before he was forced
        (A)   (B)   (C)   (D)
    to leave school.

9. I cabled them my arrival time so they could meet me at the airport.
        (A) (B)   (C)   (D)

10. In order to do well on an exam, not only should one know the required material well, but you
        (A)   (B)   (C)   (D)
    should also maintain a relaxed attitude.

11. He is said to having been an excellent opera singer in his youth.
            (A)   (B)   (C)   (D)

12. I have setted the package beside the box of geraniums on the front porch in case I have to leave
       (A)   (B)   (C)
    before you arrive.
              (D)

13. The coach said that they should have gone to the gym every day next week to get in shape for the
                       (A)   (B)   (C)   (D)
    tournament game.

14. Having served on that committee for two years, Dr. Anderson is bored of it and is looking for
       (A)   (B)   (C)
    someone to take his place.
                   (D)

15. Jane's decision will probably depend largely to her ability to find a competent person to take care of
       (A)   (B)   (C)   (D)
    her young daughter.

16.   A   bouquet of beautiful tulips were displayed in an antique vase on the large mahogany
     (A)   (B)   (C)
    dining-room table.
           (D)

17. He has been the first violinist with the London Philharmonic before he retired ten years ago.
       (A)   (B)   (C)   (D)

18. Dr. Little is planning on moving to a warmer climate as soon as he will retire next year.
                            (A)   (B)   (D)

19. The teacher asked them who had completed their tests to turn in their papers and to leave the room
                        (A)   (B)
     as quietly as possible.
    (C)   (D)

20. The native population in the northern part of the country has little opportunities to get the kind of
                                                                    (A)   (B)   (C)
    education necessary to compete in modern society.
                         (D)

21. The authorities were determined to discover the identity of the murderer, whom they feared would
                      (A)   (B)   (C)
    soon claim another innocent victim.
                (D)

22. My brother has always helped me in time of need, and I wish that he was here now.
                 (A)   (B)   (C)   (D)

23. Their free trip, which they won on a television game show, include four days in London and a
                     (A)   (B)   (C)   (D)
    Week in Paris.

GO ON TO THE NEXT PAGE

24. I <u>must</u> tell you that you looked <u>so</u> <u>handsomely</u> in your red <u>outfit</u> the other night.
     (A)   (B) (C)   (D)

25. A <u>common</u> <u>held</u> belief is that man <u>has evolved</u> from lower <u>forms</u> of life.
    (A)   (B)   (C)   (D)

Sentence Completion

Directions: In the Sentence Completion questions, one or more words are left out of each sentence. Under each sentence, you will see four words or phrases. Select the one word or phrase that completes the sentence correctly, then write it in the space provided in the book or on a separate sheet of paper.

26. One should be careful to check the grease and oil in _____ periodically.

    (A) their car
    (B) one's car
    (C) our car
    (D) your car

27. I wish I had not signed that contract without _____.

    (A) first having consulted a lawyer
    (B) not first having consulted a lawyer
    (C) first having consulted lawyer
    (D) first having consulting a lawyer

28. He likes _____ classical music on the piano.

    (A) only to play
    (B) to only play
    (C) only playing
    (D) to play only

29. The reason they are not coming is _____.

    (A) because they are angry with the hosts
    (B) that they are mad at the hosts
    (C) that they are angry with the hosts
    (D) because they are mad at the hosts

30. I went to my adviser to ask him _____.

    (A) what courses should I take
    (B) should I take what courses
    (C) I should take what courses
    (D) what courses I should take

31. He _____ before spring break.

    (A) hopes to completely finish his term paper
    (B) hopes to finish his term paper completely
    (C) hopes completely to finish his term paper
    (D) hopes to finish completely his term paper

32. Learning to do routine car maintenance oneself is often easier _____ competent people to do it.

    (A) as finding
    (B) than to find
    (C) than finding
    (D) as to find

33. Of all the sports he played, _____.

    (A) he liked tennis least
    (B) it was tennis which was his least liked
    (C) tennis was liked least by him
    (D) tennis was disliked by him most

34. _____, she was an excellent tennis player.

- (A) Because practiced constantly
- (B) She practiced constantly
- (C) Because practicing constantly
- (D) Because she practiced constantly

35. Social critics often point out the fact that the fast pace of modern life is causing people _____.

- (A) to become increasingly nervous and also even more high-strung
- (B) to become increasingly nervous and high-strung
- (C) to become increasingly nervous and to become increasingly high-strung
- (D) to increasingly become nervous and high-strung

36. That town was no longer the sleepy little village _____.

- (A) it has been being
- (B) it has been
- (C) it was
- (D) it had been

37. If we had known _____, we could have invited him to speak at our ceremonies.

- (A) whom was
- (B) who he was
- (C) who was he
- (D) he was who

38. I will meet you _____.

- (A) of the second floor
- (B) on the floor two
- (C) of the floor two
- (D) on the second floor

39. They were shipwrecked on a tiny island _____.

- (A) off the coast belonging to Japan
- (B) off of the coast of Japan
- (C) off the coast which belongs to Japan
- (D) off the coast of Japan

40. That fire yesterday _____ the whole building.

- (A) could of burned down
- (B) could have burn down
- (C) could burned down
- (D) could have burned down

Check your answers using the error key on page 180.

Error Keys

Practice Test 1

Error Identification

__(D)__   1. (*his* wanting). See Chapter 5, "Pronouns"—*Possessives*, page 85.

__(B)__   2. (*lay*). See Chapter 7, "Style"—*Usage*, page 125.

__(B)__   3. (these *kinds*). See Chapter 3, "Modifiers"—*Demonstratives*, page 27.

__(D)__   4. (*physics*). See Chapter 3, "Modifiers"—*Noun Adjectives*, page 24.

__(B)__   5. (*like*). See Chapter 3, "Modifiers"—*Sameness and Similarity*, page 31.

__(C)__   6. (*drive*). See Chapter 4, "Verbs"—*Verbals*, page 64.

__(B)__   7. (*permanence*). See Chapter 7, "Style"—*Parts of Speech*, page 144.

__(B)__   8. (*they finish*). See Chapter 4, "Verbs"—*Time Clauses*, page 56.

__(D)__   9. (three-hundred-*year*-old). See Chapter 3, "Modifiers"—*Hyphenated or Compound Adjectives*, page 26.

__(A)__   10. (*Tom had sent*). See Chapter 4, "Verbs"—*Conditionals*, page 60.

__(C)__   11. (the *younger*). See Chapter 3, "Modifiers"—*Comparatives*, page 33.

__(B)__   12. (*many*). See Chapter 3, "Modifiers"—*Few, Little, Much, and Many*, page 28.

__(B)__   13. (*to be* sleeping). See Chapter 4, "Verbs"—*Verbals*, page 64.

__(B)__   14. (*an* accurate). See Chapter 3, "Modifiers"—*Articles*, page 39.

__(D)__   15. (about the weather *constantly*). See Chapter 6, "Basic Patterns"—*Order of Adverbs*, page 100.

__(B)__   16. (*large enough*). See Chapter 3, "Modifiers"—*Too, Very, and Enough*, page 41.

__(C)__   17. (to pay for the costs of my education *completely*). See Chapter 3, "Modifiers"—*Split Infinitives*, page 18.

__(C)__   18. (*were not* stationed). See Chapter 4, "Verbs"—*Wishes*, page 64.

__(D)__   19. (*the button* broke) OR (*the needle* broke). See Chapter 5, "Pronouns"—*Faulty Reference*, page 86.

__(D)__   20. (*it was*). See Chapter 6, "Basic Patterns"—*Embedded Questions*, page 103.

__(B)__   21. (*they*). See Chapter 5, "Pronouns"—*Personal Pronouns—Case*, page 80.

__(A)__   22. (having *run*). See Chapter 4, "Verbs"—*Past Participles*, page 68.

__(B)__   23. (*no* longer). See Chapter 3, "Modifiers"—*Negation*, page 43.

__(A)__   24. (*having*). See Chapter 4, "Verbs"—*Verbals*, page 64.

__(B)__   25. (*me*). See Chapter 5, "Pronouns"—*Personal Pronouns—Case*, page 80.

Sentence Completion

__(A)__   26. (A) **Correct**
              (B) See Chapter 3, "Modifiers"—*Cause and Result*, page 37.
              (C) See Chapter 3, "Modifiers"—*Cause and Result*, page 37.
              (D) See Chapter 3, "Modifiers"—*Cause and Result*, page 37.

__(C)__   27. (A) See Chapter 3, "Modifiers"—*Demonstratives*, page 27.
              (B) See Chapter 7, "Style"—*Usage*, page 125.
              (C) **Correct**
              (D) Same as A and B

__(C)__   28. (A) See Chapter 7, "Style"—*Correlative Conjunctions*, page 139.
              (B) See Chapter 7, "Style"—*Correlative Conjunctions*, page 139.
              (C) **Correct**
              (D) See Chapter 7, "Style"—*Correlative Conjunctions*, page 139.

__(B)__ **29.** (A) See Chapter 6, "Basic Patterns"— *Clauses*, page 107.
　　 (B) **Correct**
　　 (C) See Chapter 6, "Basic Patterns"— *Clauses*, page 107.
　　 (D) See Chapter 6, "Basic Patterns"— *Clauses*, page 107.

__(D)__ **30.** (A) See Chapter 7, "Style"—*Prepositions in Combinations*, page 46.
　　 (B) See Chapter 7, "Style"—*Prepositions in Combinations*, page 46.
　　 (C) See Chapter 7, "Style"—*Prepositions in Combinations*, page 46.
　　 (D) **Correct**

__(C)__ **31.** (A) See Chapter 4, "Verbs"— *Conditionals*, page 60.
　　 (B) See Chapter 4, "Verbs"— *Conditionals*, page 60.
　　 (C) **Correct**
　　 (D) See Chapter 4, "Verbs"— *Conditionals*, page 60.

__(B)__ **32.** (A) See Chapter 3, "Modifiers"— *Too, Very, and Enough*, page 41.
　　 (B) **Correct**
　　 (C) See Chapter 3, "Modifiers"— *Too, Very, and Enough*, page 41.
　　 (D) See Chapter 3, "Modifiers"— *Too, Very, and Enough*, page 41.

__(A)__ **33.** (A) **Correct**
　　 (B) See Chapter 7, "Style"—*Prepositions in Combinations*, page 46.
　　 (C) See Chapter 7, "Style"—*Prepositions in Combinations*, page 46.
　　 (D) Same as A. See also Chapter 4, "Verbs"—*Verbals*, page 64.

__(B)__ **34.** (A) See Chapter 5, "Pronouns"— *Personal Pronouns—Case*, page 80.
　　 (B) **Correct**
　　 (C) See Chapter 5, "Pronouns"— *Personal Pronouns—Case*, page 80.
　　 (D) See Chapter 5, "Pronouns"— *Personal Pronouns—Case*, page 80.

__(B)__ **35.** (A) See Chapter 5, "Pronouns"— *Faulty Reference*, page 86.
　　 (B) **Correct**

　　 (C) Same as A. See also Chapter 7, "Style"—*Parallelism*, page 117.
　　 (D) See Chapter 6, "Basic Patterns"— *Order of Adverbs*, page 100.

__(D)__ **36.** (A) See Chapter 4, "Verbs"— *Wishes*, page 59.
　　 (B) Incorrect negative formation (*did not live*)
　　 (C) See Chapter 4, "Verbs"— *Wishes*, page 59.
　　 (D) **Correct**

__(B)__ **37.** (A) See Chapter 7, "Style"—*Wordiness*, page 120.
　　 (B) **Correct**
　　 (C) Same as A
　　 (D) Same as A. See also Chapter 7, "Style"—*Voice*, page 115.

__(A)__ **38.** (A) **Correct**
　　 (B) See Chapter 5, "Pronouns"— *Those* Modified, page 92.
　　 (C) Same as B
　　 (D) *See* Chapter 7, "Style"—*Wordiness*, page 120.

__(D)__ **39.** (A) See Chapter 4, "Verbs"—*Tense*, page 55.
　　 (B) See Chapter 4, "Verbs"—*Tense*, page 55.
　　 (C) See Chapter 4, "Verbs"—*Tense*, page 55.
　　 (D) **Correct**

__(A)__ **40.** (A) **Correct**
　　 (B) See Chapter 6, "Basic Patterns"— *To/For (Purpose)*, page 105.
　　 (C) See Chapter 6, "Basic Patterns"— *To/For (Purpose)*, page 105.
　　 (D) See Chapter 6, "Basic Patterns"— *To/For (Purpose)*, page 105.

Practice Test 2

Error Identification

_(A)_   1. (*lost* respect). See Chapter 3, "Modifiers"—*Articles*, page 39.

_(A)_   2. (*whether*). See Chapter 7, "Style"—*Words Often Confused*, Group III, page 137.

_(D)_   3. (might *have* enjoyed). See Chapter 4, "Verbs"—*Conditionals*, page 60.

_(A)_   4. (*Since Howard did not pass the law exam,*). See Chapter 3, "Modifiers"—*Dangling Modifiers*, page 19.

_(A)_   5. (*interestingly*). See Chapter 3, "Modifiers"—*Adjective/Adverb Confusion*, page 21.

_(D)_   6. (*anywhere*). See Chapter 7, "Style"—*Substandard*, page 122.

_(A)_   7. (*I reserved*). See Chapter 4, "Verbs"—*Tense*, page 55.

_(C)_   8. (*and an*). See Chapter 7, "Style"—*Parallelism*, page 117.

_(D)_   9. (*without rain*). See Chapter 3, "Modifiers"—*Negation*, page 43.

_(A)_   10. (such *a* difficult time). See Chapter 3, "Modifiers"—*Cause and Result*, page 37.

_(B)_   11. (*make*). See Chapter 4, "Verbs"—*Verbals*, page 64.

_(C)_   12. (*whoever*). See Chapter 5, "Pronouns"—*Who/Whom*, page 83.

_(A)_   13. (*between*). See Chapter 7, "Style"—*Usage*, page 125.

_(A)_   14. (*who*). See Chapter 5, "Pronouns"—*Relative Pronouns*, page 79.

_(A)_   15. (*these*). See Chapter 3, "Modifiers"—*Demonstratives*, page 27.

_(D)_   16. (*Henry's*). See Chapter 3, "Modifiers"—*Comparatives*, page 33.

_(C)_   17. (*to catch*). See Chapter 6, "Basic Patterns"—*To/For (Purpose)*, page 105.

_(B)_   18. (*so* satisfying). See Chapter 3, "Modifiers"—*Cause and Result*, page 37.

_(C)_   19. (gate *one*). See Chapter 3, "Modifiers"—*Cardinal and Ordinal Numbers*, page 30.

_(B)_   20. (has *risen*). See Chapter 7, "Style"—*Usage*, page 125.

_(B)_   21. (*turn off*). See Chapter 4, "Verbs—*Verbs of "Demand,"* page 57.

_(B)_   22. (*quite*). See Chapter 7, "Style"—*Words Often Confused*, Group II, page 129.

_(A)_   23. (*tired*). See Chapter 3, "Modifiers"—*Adjectives after Verbs of Sensation*, page 23.

_(C)_   24. (*still* has not returned). See Chapter 6, "Basic Patterns"—*Order of Adverbs*, page 100.

_(C)_   25. (*sat*). See Chapter 7, "Style"—*Usage*, page 125.

Sentence Completion

_(D)_   26. (A) See Chapter 7, "Style"—*Subject/Verb Agreement*, page 141.
     (B) See Chapter 3, "Modifiers"—*Few, Little, Much,* and *Many*, page 28.
     (C) Same as A and B
     (D) **Correct**

_(B)_   27. (A) See Chapter 5, "Pronouns"—*Relative Pronouns*, page 79.
     (B) **Correct**
     (C) See Chapter 5, "Pronouns"—*Relative Pronouns*, page 79.
     (D) See Chapter 5, "Pronouns"—*Relative Pronouns*, page 79.

_(A)_   28. (A) **Correct**
     (B) See Chapter 4, "Verbs"—*Tense*, page 55., and Chapter 3, "Modifiers"—*Adjectives after Verbs of Sensation*, page 23.
     (C) Same as B
     (D) See Chapter 4, "Verbs"—*Tense*, page 55.

_(C)_ **29.** (A) See Chapter 3, "Modifiers"—
  Noun Adjectives, page 24.
  (B) See Chapter 3, "Modifiers"—
  Noun Adjectives, page 24.
  (C) **Correct**
  (D) See Chapter 3, "Modifiers"—
  Noun Adjectives, page 24.

_(B)_ **30.** (A) See Chapter 4, "Verbs"—
  Verbals, page 64.
  (B) **Correct**
  (C) See Chapter 4, "Verbs"—
  Verbals, page 64.
  (D) See Chapter 4, "Verbs"—
  Verbals, page 64.

_(A)_ **31.** (A) **Correct**
  (B) See Chapter 6, "Basic Patterns"—
  Indirect Objects, page 99.
  (C) Same as B
  (D) Same as B

_(D)_ **32.** (A) See Chapter 7, "Style"—_Wordiness_, page 120.
  (B) Same as A
  (C) Same as A
  (D) **Correct**

_(C)_ **33.** (A) See Chapter 7, "Style"—_Words Often Confused_, Group I, page 44.
  (B) Same as A. See also Chapter 4, "Verbs"—_Verbs of "Demand,"_ page 57, and Chapter 7, "Style"—_Usage_, page 125.
  (C) **Correct**
  (D) See Chapter 4, "Verbs"—_Verbs of "Demand,"_ page 57. See also Chapter 7, "Style"—_Usage_ page 125.

_(C)_ **34.** (A) See Chapter 4, "Verbs"—_Modals_, page 62.
  (B) Same as A
  (C) **Correct**
  (D) Same as A

_(C)_ **35.** (A) See Chapter 6, "Basic Patterns"—_Double Subjects_, page 106.
  (B) See Chapter 6, "Basic Patterns"—_Clauses_, page 107.
  (C) **Correct**
  (D) Same as B

_(C)_ **36.** (A) See Chapter 7, "Style"—_Parallelism_, page 117.
  (B) Same as A
  (C) **Correct**
  (D) Same as A

_(A)_ **37.** (A) **Correct**
  (B) See Chapter 4, "Verbs"—_Verbs of "Demand,"_ page 57.
  (C) Same as B
  (D) Same as B

_(C)_ **38.** (A) See Chapter 3, "Modifiers"—_Comparatives_, page 33.
  (B) Same as A
  (C) **Correct**
  (D) Same as A

_(D)_ **39.** (A) See Chapter 3, "Modifiers"—_Adjective/Adverb Confusion_, page 21.
  (B) See Chapter 4, "Verbs"—_Conditionals_, page 60.
  (C) See Chapter 3, "Modifiers"—_Comparatives_, page 33.
  (D) **Correct**

_(C)_ **40.** (A) See Chapter 5, "Pronouns"—_Number_, page 89.
  (B) See Chapter 5, "Pronouns"—_Person_, page 88.
  (C) **Correct**
  (D) See Chapter 5

PRACTICE TEST 3

Error Identification

_(C)_ **1.** (_changing_). See Chapter 4, "Verbs"—_Verbals_, page 64.

_(A)_ **2.** (_custom is_). See Chapter 6, "Basic Patterns"—_Double Subjects_, page 106.

_(C)_ **3.** (but _also_). See Chapter 7, "Style"—_Correlative Conjunctions_, page 139.

_(B)_ **4.** (Kathy studies _hard in the library_ night and day). See Chapter 7, "Style"—_Voice_, page 115.

_(D)_ **5.** (_its_). See Chapter 5, "Pronouns"—_Number_, page 89.

___(B)___ 6. (gave *his* advisers). See Chapter 6, "Basic Patterns"—*Indirect Objects*, page 99.

___(B)___ 7. (was *better*). See Chapter 3, "Modifiers"—*Comparatives*, page 33.

___(B)___ 8. (was able to finish *only* one semester). See Chapter 3, "Modifiers"—*Adverbs like Only*, page 17.

___(C)___ 9. (*so that*). See Chapter 7, "Style"—*Words Often Confused*, Group III, page 137.

___(D)___ 10. (*one* should) OR (*he* should). See Chapter 5, "Pronouns"—*Person*, page 88.

___(B)___ 11. (*have* been). See Chapter 4, "Verbs"—*Present and Perfect Participles and Infinitives*, page 71.

___(A)___ 12. (have *set*). See Chapter 4, "Verbs"—*Past Participles*, page 68. See also Chapter 7, "Style"—*Usage*, page 125.

___(B)___ 13. (should *go*). See Chapter 4, "Verbs"—*Modals*, page 62.

___(C)___ 14. (bored *with* it). See Chapter 7, "Style"—*Prepositions in Combinations*, page 46.

___(B)___ 15. (largely *on*). See Chapter 7, "Style"—*Prepositions in Combinations*, page 46.

___(B)___ 16. (*was* displayed). See Chapter 7, "Style"—*Subject/Verb Agreement*, page 141.

___(A)___ 17. (*had been* OR *was*). See Chapter 4, "Verbs"—*Tense*, page 55.

___(D)___ 18. (he *retires*). See Chapter 4, "Verbs"—*Time Clauses*, page 56.

___(A)___ 19. (*those*). See Chapter 5, "Pronouns"—*Those Modified*, page 92.

___(A)___ 20. (*few*). See Chapter 3, "Modifiers"—*Few, Little, Much, and Many*, page 28.

___(C)___ 21. (*who*). See Chapter 5, "Pronouns"—*Who/Whom*, page 83.

___(D)___ 22. (*were*). See Chapter 4, "Verbs"—*Wishes*, page 59.

___(C)___ 23. (*includes*). See Chapter 7, "Style"—*Subject/Verb Agreement*, page 141.

___(C)___ 24. (*handsome*). See Chapter 3, "Modifiers"—*Adjectives After Verbs of Sensation*, page 23.

___(A)___ 25. (*commonly*). See Chapter 3, "Modifiers"—*Adjective/Adverb Confusion*, page 21.

Sentence Completion

___(B)___ 26. (A) See Chapter 5, "Pronouns"—*Number*, page 89.
         (B) **Correct**
         (C) See Chapter 5, "Pronouns"—*Person*, page 88.
         (D) Same as C

___(A)___ 27. (A) **Correct**
         (B) See Chapter 3, "Modifiers"—*Negation*, page 43.
         (C) See Chapter 3, "Modifiers"—*Articles*, page 39.
         (D) See Chapter 4, "Verbs"—*Present and Perfect Participles and Infinitives*, page 71.

___(D)___ 28. (A) See Chapter 3, "Modifiers"—*Adverbs like Only*, page 17.
         (B) See Chapter 3, "Modifiers"—*Split Infinitives*, page 18.
         (C) Same as A
         (D) **Correct**

___(C)___ 29. (A) See Chapter 7, "Style"—*Substandard*, page 122.
         (B) Same as A
         (C) **Correct**
         (D) Same as A

___(D)___ 30. (A) See Chapter 6, "Basic Patterns"—*Embedded Questions*, page 103.
         (B) Same as A
         (C) Same as A
         (D) **Correct**

___(B)___ 31. (A) See Chapter 3, "Modifiers"—*Split Infinitives*, page 18.
         (B) **Correct**
         (C) See Chapter 6, "Basic Patterns"—*Order of Adverbs*, page 100.
         (D) Same as C

__(C)__ 32. (A) See Chapter 3, "Modifiers"—
Comparatives, page 33.
(B) See Chapter 7, "Style"—*Paral-lelism*, page 117.
(C) **Correct**
(D) Same as A and B.

__(A)__ 33. (A) **Correct**
(B) See Chapter 7, "Style"—*Wordi-ness*, page 120.
(C) See Chapter 7, "Style"—*Voice*, page 115.
(D) Same as B

__(D)__ 34. (A) See Chapter 6, "Basic Patterns"—
Clauses, page 107.
(B) Same as A
(C) Same as A
(D) **Correct**

__(B)__ 35. (A) See Chapter 7, "Style"—*Wordi-ness*, page 120.
(B) **Correct**
(C) Same as A
(D) See Chapter 3, "Modifiers"—
Split Infinitives, page 18.

__(D)__ 36. (A) See Chapter 4, "Verbs"—*Tense*, page 55.
(B) Same as A
(C) Same as A
(D) **Correct**

__(B)__ 37. (A) See Chapter 5, "Pronouns"—
Who/Whom, page 83.
(B) **Correct**
(C) See Chapter 6, "Basic Patterns"—
Embedded Questions, page 103.
(D) Same as C

__(D)__ 38. (A) See Chapter 7, "Style"—*Prepo-sitions* (*General Use*), page 146.
(B) See Chapter 3, "Modifiers"—
Cardinal and Ordinal Numbers, page 30.
(C) Same as A and B
(D) **Correct**

__(D)__ 39. (A) See Chapter 7, "Style"—*Wordi-ness*, page 120.
(B) See Chapter 7, "Style"—*Substan-dard*, page 122.
(C) Same as A
(D) **Correct**

__(D)__ 40. (A) See Chapter 4, "Verbs"—
Modals, page 64.
(B) See Chapter 4, "Verbs"—*Past Participles*, page 68.
(C) Same as A
(D) **Correct**

NOTES

NOTES

NOTES